Driving Change

Driving Change

Techniques for improving your personal and professional performance

William Fintan Bohan

Strategic Book Publishing and Rights Co.

Strategic Book Publishing & Rights Co., LLC
USA | Singapore
www.sbpra.net

For information about special discounts for bulk purchases, please contact Strategic Book Publishing and Rights Co. Special Sales, at bookorder@sbpra.net.

ISBN: 978-1-68235-548-0

I dedicate this book to my children, Eamon, Liam and Tessa. The first incarnation of this text was titled "What I wish I had known when I was 25 years old", an attempt to write a short manual for them to accelerate their careers.

Contents

J.W. Goethe: "The only man who never makes a mistake is he who never does anything."

PROLOGUE

M ore than a decade ago at a social event, a friend mentioned that he knew "a gringo consultant with an unusual method of helping companies to increase profits". Smiling, I told him that I had a lot of experience with consultants of that type because, in my work at a large Latin American airline, I had to lead improvement processes with consultancies that promised significant results. I also explained that I was dissatisfied with their methodologies, for three reasons: first, they are based on multiple questionnaires with different people who usually say what they think the consultant wants; second, they focus on reducing costs, which means most of the time firing people; and third, the end result is a nice folder full of recommendations that usually ends up on a VP´s bookshelf. And none of that translated into action.

My friend then told me that Fintan's method (that was the gringo´s name) was different and offered to introduce us. After many long conversations, during which we shared our professional and personal experiences, Fintan handed me a business novel that he had written so that I could better understand his methodology. The title was quite decisive: "The Hidden Power of Productivity" with the sub-title, "How to improve productivity by 30%, without having to fire anyone!"

After reading it, Fintan´s philosophy of life became very clear to me, explained with great transparency in his novel. The book describes how to help businesses grow through people. To make a long story short, I offered to Fintan that I invest in Trinity as a partner. From 2013 to now, we have had excellent experiences with clients in different countries and cultures, and better still, I have learnt an authentic way of helping people to grow, while being able to make a good living from it!

During this journey, I got my hands on another book by Fintan, which I wished I had read many years earlier: "Double productivity in your Start-up". Indeed, what Fintan proposes in this book are measures that allow us to face the problems of every entrepreneur, in a simple and easily understandable way. Better still, with concrete and measurable results.

I am so happy that Fintan decided to take advantage of the pandemic lockdown to capture his experiences in this new book that I am sure will be the perfect complement to the other two, and at the same time, a practical guide to help all of us who will have to reinvent ourselves as a result of the changes that we have all experienced and that have opened our eyes to something inevitable: change will carry on happening. Thus, "Driving change" should become indispensable material for all those who know that, in our fast-moving world, the only constant is change (Heraclitus).

Our environment has changed, and for better or worse, people and organizations are challenged to incorporate into their daily lives the adaptation and transformation to new realities, as a constant over time.

Raul Ponce
Chief Executive Officer
Trinity Profits & People

01

Introduction to Change

You are either driving change, or you are being driven by change:

Which is it to be?

Starting in 2020, things changed quickly. A world-wide pandemic forced change upon 7 billion people.

A long period of relative PERCEIVED stability came to an end.

There is no return to the "normality" of 2019.

Some people say that we will eventually return to "normality". that's hopeful thinking, but unrealistic. The new normality is that Change will increase, and at an ever-increasing rate.

The last great pandemic was the Spanish flu, from 1918 to 1920. Based on this evidence alone, you might assume that we will not see another global pandemic for another 100 years or so, but that is a risky assumption.

World population (approx.)	1920	2020
	1.9 billion	7.7 billion

The increasing interaction with animals and humans will only speed up the mutation of cross-species viruses.

Most of us reading this book will be alive when these upcoming changes occur:

- another pandemic
- climate change: either it happens, or we control it
- genetic engineering in humans
- artificial intelligence surpassing human intelligence
- interplanetary travel
- confirmation of UFOs
- a major earthquake
- a major financial crash
- a surprise no one saw coming.

At some point in your life, you have probably felt a sudden tightness in the stomach, a wave of anxiety flowing over you, your breath becoming shallow. Perhaps you were summoned unexpectedly to your boss' office, at an unusual time.

Perhaps you received an unexpected phone call, and the voice on the other side says: "I have something to tell you".

You sensed that a change was coming.

Even though we know intellectually that change is inevitable, we have been conditioned by society to prefer stability and security.

The fundamental truth of reality is that change is the only true constant.

By conditioning ourselves into the habit of adapting to many micro-changes, we are better able to emotionally accept major changes. Instead of resisting change, we flow alongside it, we are part of it.

This book seeks to offer you a mindset for taking hold of the rudder of change in your life, and your business. It will provide you with practical ideas and tools for change, both personally and professionally.

Let's heed what the Daleks frequently say to Dr. Who: "resistance is useless". Resisting change is indeed futile – get used to change and BE A PART OF IT. Constantly.

Image of a Dalek, an extraterrestrial mutant race from the BBC science fiction series, *Doctor Who*

02

The SABRe Model for Changing Results

"Insanity is doing the same thing over and over again, but expecting different results," a quote repeatedly misattributed to Einstein, which is somewhat ironic. Many people overlook the fact that if we want to generate an improved result in our lives, we need to change something about ourselves.

A powerful tool for change is the SABRe model. The SABRe model refers to **S**ystems, **A**ttitudes, **B**ehaviors and **Re**sults.

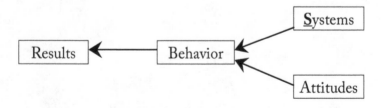

This model describes the change process, whether it be a Quality program, a Safety program, or a Company-wide productivity improvement program. It is also useful in the context of personal productivity improvement.

If we wish to change our own personal or professional RESULTS, then what we must change what we DO which generates those RESULTS: in other words, our behavior.

For example: imagine you weigh 100 kgs, and you wish to run a marathon, so you consult your doctor. Your doctor tells you that your current exercise regime of walking 1 kilometer per day is not enough. And he calculates that you consume on average 2.200 calories per day. These **Results** are your BASE LINE.

Your doctor suggests to you that maintaining the same eating and exercise habits will not generate the **Future Result** you desire. He proposes these TARGETS, which you accept:

a) weight 81 kgs
b) eat less than 2.000 calories per day
c) minimum of 5 kilometers per day.

Note that a) is the end RESULT, while b) and c) are the new BEHAVIORS. But changing a behavior from one day to another is often easier said than done.

There are two useful levers we can pull in order to help us change our behavior.

The first lever is our SYSTEMS, in other words, how we manage ourselves. What measurements, methods, procedures, structures, etc. that we use to plan, schedule, implement, control and report on our performance. A saying goes: "you do not get what you *expect*, you get what you *inspect*." Another well-known saying indicates: "*If you cannot measure it, it does not exist.*"

So, following this example, you purchase a bathroom scale and measure your weight every morning and show it on a graph. You also record how many kilometers you jog or walk, and graph that. And you keep a calorie count of what you eat. After a while, you find this feedback motivational.

The second lever is our ATTITUDES. We need to examine our beliefs and thought patterns, and consciously change them when we detect that they are debilitating us.

For example, the automatic thought "*I never will be able to do a marathon*" does not help you. Better is to choose to replace this thought whenever it comes up with: "*I can do anything I set my mind to.*" Read motivational literature, meet with your running group, and listen to motivational Ted Talks on the way to work. Consciously feed your mind with positive thoughts.

Whether we are working on quality, safety, professional or personal productivity, the steps are as follows:

RESULTS

1. Identify and QUANTIFY our Result today which we wish to improve. This is our BASE LINE.
2. Set a TARGET Result and define WHEN it should be achieved.

BEHAVIORS

3. Identify our CURRENT behaviors, which produce our current Base Line Result.
4. Identify the new DESIRED BEHAVIORS, which will generate the TARGET Result.

SYSTEMS

5. Define what we need to measure, and at what frequency.

ATTITUDES

6. Identify current unconscious thought patterns and examine whether they allow you to grow or whether they hold you back. Choose another set of thought patterns. Choose the vehicle for inputting these thoughts into your nervous system.

In following chapters, we will cover Systems, Behaviors and Attitudes in more depth.

03

The Japanese term, "Muda"

The Japanese word MUDA came to international fame when used as an integral part of the Toyota Production System (TPS). The word is loosely translated as "waste, useless". In the TPS, it refers to any activity or process or resource which DOES NOT ADD VALUE to the product or service we supply to **OUR CLIENTS**. Nowadays, it appears as simple and common sense. But only 40 years ago, it represented a great PARADIGM change. A paradigm shift which allowed Toyota to overtake the Big Three from the US as the world's main car manufacturer.

This is an example of the power of applying a new paradigm.

During the 1980´s, Western car manufacturers considered the time changing the production line from one model to another as PRODUCTIVE time. This is understandable, because the technicians work hard, and a production line does not change itself. The changeover would usually take several shifts to complete, say 24 hours work. Consequently, western manufacturers were obliged to program long production runs, thereby absorbing the changeover cost into a large volume, and hence reducing the unit cost of a car. The paradigm in western companies was: how can we produce faster?

The Japanese paradigm was different. While they recognized that changeovers are necessary, they decided that they are MUDA. In other words, a change-over does not add more value to any client, since while it occurs, no car is being made to fulfill a customer need. They therefore decided to reduce the changeover time. Instead of looking to make the production process faster, they looked at trying to minimize the non-value adding time. They succeeded. Typical changeover times were reduced by more than 90%.

	Example of Production Changes from a Paradigm Shift			
		West	Japan	% improvement
A	Line changeover time (hours)	24	2	-92%
B	Nominal Production rate (cars / hour)	90	90	
C	Economic production batch size (stock of cars)	3400	2100	-38%
D	Hours to produce production batch D = C / B	37,8	23,3	
E	TOTAL production line hours C = A + B	61,8	25,3	-59%
		This represents quicker delivery time		
F	Average NET production rate (cars / hour) F = C / E	55,0	82,9	51%

In the above example, notice that work-in-progress inventory levels drop by 38% (C), delivery time is quicker by 59% (E), and overall productivity increases by 51% (F).

This innovation / paradigm shift allowed the Japanese to produce shorter production runs, and hence respond more quickly to customer demand. It also allowed them to rapidly kill off a product which was not popular with customers, instead of filling massive parking lots with unsold inventory. The example most often quoted of an overproduction of cars which did not sell is the Ford Edsel *(https://en.wikipedia.org/wiki/Edsel)*.

Since then, the concept has been applied to every industry and service area imaginable. It is also applicable to individuals, like you, dear reader.

Please accept the definitions below for the purposes of the remainder of this book.

MUDA in Companies:

*"Anythingb which fails to **ADD VALUE** to the product or service for the **CLIENT**."*

PERSONAL Muda:

*"Anything which does not **ADD VALUE** to the realization of my **PERSONAL GOALS** or dreams."*

04

A definition of "Performance"

If you asked 100 managers, "How do you define performance?", you would receive a wide variety of responses.

We must sing from the same songbook. Therefore, for the purposes of this book, I propose this definition. High business performance is achieved with a combination of these 5 factors:

- optimal Safety - the care and well-being of all your dependents and yourself
- optimal Quality - compliance with specifications promised to the customer
- optimal Productivity - the achievement of production goals with the effective use of resources.
- optimal work environment - the role of a good Supervisor - Boss – or Manager includes knowing and managing the feelings of his people.

- optimal Customer Service - achievement of the 4 above leads to an optimal level of Customer Service.

Some people think that by emphasizing productivity, we put quality or safety at risk. They think that the quest to get things done more quickly induces more errors due to haste and more accidents for the same reason.

This thinking is wrong. High productivity DOES NOT MEAN working in a rush. Rather, it means working CALMLY.

Napoleon Bonaparte is widely regarded as a military genius and one of the greatest commanders in world history. In the 20 years of his military career, he fought more than 70 battles, losing only eight, most at the end with the unfortunate decision to invade Russia during the winter

Napoleon was famous for leading his troops from the front. He took great care in his appearance as the leader and motivator of his people, and put particular attention into his military uniform, knowing that a careless detail in his appearance would affect the perception of his soldiers. For this reason, he instructed his butler, when the latter was helping to put on his uniform:

"Dress me slowly, for I am in a hurry."

Napoleon knew that: MORE CALM LEADS TO GREATER PRODUCTIVITY.

AND MORE CALM can only be achieved with very good PLANNING.

To Summarize:

A High-Performance Supervisor knows that he cannot be productive if the environment is unsafe. He also knows that a decline in quality is a decline in productivity. High-Performance Supervisors know that the best way to work is to do it right the first time, that's why they get:

- Optimal Security
- Optimal Quality
- Optimal Productivity
- Within an optimal climate or work environment

As a consequence of achieving these 4 points, High-Performance Supervisors achieve an excellent level of Customer Service.

05

Setting personal goals

Question: *Mahatma Gandhi, Charlie Chaplin, Bill Gates, Steve Jobs, Mother Teresa, Nelson Mandela, Jesus Christ, Martin Luther King, Henry Ford.* What do they all have in common?

Answer: Every one of them contributed positively to changing the world, starting with little or zero capital.

Question: How did they achieve this?

Answer: They all committed to crystal-clear goals.

Freeing India, making people laugh, a computer on every desktop, relief for the extreme poor, freedom in South Africa, living through love and not fear, equality in the USA, affordable personal transport for the working man: in every case they had a clear, committed and non-negotiable personal goal.

As business professionals, we often think that productivity applies only in our workplaces. Rarely do we look at "Personal Productivity", while "Professional Productivity" gets plenty of attention. The latter is easier to understand; as an employee of a company, your professional productivity can be measured by what you achieve, or the proportion of your time that you dedicate to those activities which help achieve your Company's Mission, or generate value added for your clients or customers. Your Company has a stated goal or Mission, and how productive you are at work depends on how well you help your Company achieve its goal or Mission.

But can we measure productivity on a personal level? A hint: our personal productivity reflects how well we are working (or not!) towards our PERSONAL GOALS. This presupposes that we are clear on what our personal goals are. If not, our personal productivity is zero. The lack of personal goals is equivalent to zero personal productivity.

In his audio program, the "Psychology of Achievement", Brian Tracy refers to a study conducted at Yale University in 1953. That year, the graduating students were asked: *do you have clear, written personal goals for what you want to do with the rest of your life, now that you have graduated?* Surprisingly, only 3% said, "YES!" In other words, 97% of the graduates from one of America's premier universities *__did not__* have clear personal goals.

This may seem like some interesting but irrelevant statistic, were it not for what happened afterwards. Twenty years later, in 1973, the surviving graduates were tracked down and interviewed. The researchers uncovered a startling statistic: the net financial worth of the 3% who had clear declared goals exceeded that of the other 97% combined!

You may think: "surely, that is not conclusive evidence. It is only anecdotal evidence at best." Other people may think: "isn't measuring financial goals a very narrow-minded way of looking at human achievement?"

For anecdotal evidence, we have already mentioned Mahatma Gandhi, Charlie Chaplin, Bill Gates, Mother Teresa, Nelson Mandela, Jesus Christ, Martin Luther King, and Henry Ford as examples of people who had set clear-cut goals, and as a result, positively changed the world.

Regarding financial goals, the people listed above did not start out with financial goals, even though at least 3 became multi-millionaires. Their goals were somewhat higher and more intangible: freedom, laughter, banishment of poverty, brotherly love, a computer on every desk, a car priced for everyone's budget. Their driving force was not fame or fortune, but the goal itself. All of them worked hard pursuing their goals: the fame and the wealth were by-products.

Another long-range study bears this out, this time from Harvard University. In this case, Harvard asked 1,500 graduating students of their MBA course what they wished to do with their lives. Some 83% declared "*make money*". The remaining 17% stated, "*make a valuable contribution*". Some 10 years later, the students were re-interviewed. The result? 101 had become millionaires. The most striking finding was that 100 of the 101 millionaires came from the 17%!

There is enough anecdotal or role-model evidence to indicate that goal setting is a very powerful process for any human being. After all, how can you achieve goals if you don't set them?

Goals mean growth. Growth means change. Change means pain. Change and pain are integral, inescapable parts of nature and of life. People with clear goals can better withstand pain in the search for a high ideal.

This is an effort which you should make as a gift to yourself. No-one else can do this for you. Start now.

The rest of this book will help you develop this, perhaps the most important effort of your life.

06

Questions to help you identify your personal goals

In his highly acclaimed audio motivational program, "The Psychology of Achievement", Brian Tracy recommends that we ask ourselves these following 7 questions in order to identify the true driving passion that resides within each one of us. Take no more than 10 minutes to work through them all. You are looking for the answer from the heart, not an intellectual answer from the head, and so, your first "gut-feel" response is usually the best.

1. What are the 5 things you most value in life? What you would pay more for, die for, fight for?
2. In 30 seconds or less, write down the 3 most important goals you currently have in your life.
3. What would you do if you won or were gifted US$10 million? If you had all the time and money in the world, how would you spend it? What changes would you make in your life?

4. How would you spend your time if today you were told that you only had 6 months to live?
5. What have you always wanted to do, but been afraid to try?
6. Looking back on your life, what activities or circumstances have given you the greatest sense of satisfaction, achievement, and sense of wellbeing?
7. The Genie of the Lamp appears to you and grants you one wish. What would you wish for, knowing that you could absolutely NOT fail?

Your answers to these questions point to what you would do or have if there were no mental, physical, financial or time limitations. Anything that you can conceive, you can achieve, as Napoleon Hill stated. The key is how intensely you desire it and how willing you are to invest the time and effort to achieve it.

If your answers to questions 2 and 3 do not coincide with what you would do if you only had 6 months to live (question 4), then it is vitally important that you rethink your goals, because this answer shows what you truly value in your life.

For question 5, consider what holds you back from this: often, it is a conditioned response, a fear of failure, rather than reality.

After answering these questions, choose the central, dominating purpose to your life. Not selecting a defining purpose in life also is a CHOICE!

This exercise is individual. It is your responsibility entirely. You CANNOT delegate this to anyone. The only person who can oversee the rudder of your life is you: whether you choose or not a direction to aim your rudder is entirely your responsibility. This means that you have no-one else to blame but yourself for your failure to set a central, dominating purpose to your life.

Do yourself a favor: Set a central and dominating purpose in your life.

07

Firing up your peak personal performance

Here is a sure-fire recipe for *never* getting to the peak of your personal productivity:

- stay for months or even years in a job that does not arouse any passion in you.
- stay for months or even years in a job without taking the DECISION to be passionate about what you do.

Many people spend their working lives doing a job just to fill in time until they can do what they really enjoy at the weekend. They look upon their jobs as a sacrifice that they must endure so that they can pay for what they really enjoy. They devote 8 to 10 hours of their lives each day to work in jobs they don't like, for bosses they don't respect, producing or selling products or services they don't care about.

Here are some danger signs that you may be in the wrong job:

a. When you are not actively interested in learning more about your job or your field.
b. If you don't have the inner desire to be outstanding at your job.
c. When you are not constantly learning and growing in your field, your value to your current employer and any future potential employer diminishes.
d. If you think that it is enough to do your current job to an averagely acceptable level and that, when the right job comes along, *then* you will really put your head down and do a good job.

Somehow, the "right job" never comes along. The reality is that, because of a negative or passive attitude, many people miss out on promotion and advancement. They usually stay at the same level, even if they move from company to company, or from job to job. What is more, over time, they may come to resent others for their advancement, and / or blame their bosses for their own lack of progress.

If you are a manager and you suspect that some of your team may belong to this group, what can you do to help them?

The Bible says, "A prophet is never accepted in his own land." Meaning that there are certain things that they will never believe from you, simply because it is you who is talking, and of course, in their perception, you have a vested interest in keeping them down. It's all your fault, remember?

So, you can bring in someone credible from outside to deliver a message. The message is this:

Like it or not, the fact is that you are who you are, and where you are, because you have chosen so. If you have not **consciously** chosen personal goals for yourself, if you merely drifted into this job through chance, then that has been your choice, unconsciously. Nobody forced you. Nobody can change your situation but yourself. The goal of any company is to serve its customers to the highest quality at the lowest price possible. Therefore, the company will correctly seek to hire people at the lowest possible cost. There is no obligation for anyone to pay you any more than you are now getting.

If you are serious about wanting to move up in your company, then it is **your responsibility** to become very good, even excellent, at what you do.

People who are unsuccessful and unhappy in their work are those who have not taken the time to deal honestly and openly with themselves. They have not looked deep within to find their inner treasures of talent and ability. They are content to do work that other people design and to achieve **other people's goals**.

If any of this rings true for you, how can you change this?

Decide on the **goals** for your life which light your passion. If you are not passionate about your job, then **decide** to be so! If not, find another job where you come to life! Be passionate, and then train yourself to be excellent!

Success comes from being excellent. Companies pay excellent rewards for excellent performance, average rewards for average performance and below-average rewards and insecurity for below-average performance. Many people either fail to choose to be excellent at their job or fail to change their job. As such, their implicit choice is NEVER to be successful.

Highly successful and happy people know in their hearts that they are very good at what they do. When you are doing what you really love and enjoy, if you are following your true passion, you will know because of your attitude. When you are following your passion, you will go any distance, pay any price, and overcome any obstacle to develop yourself to the point where you are world-class.

When you find your true passion, you will have a continuous desire to learn more about it. Then you throw your whole heart into doing what you do in an excellent fashion.

Therefore, the message is: CHOOSE to be excellent at your job or CHOOSE to change it.

08

Balancing your goals for personal productivity

There is a saying: "Time is Money". Not only is this saying grossly harmful, it is incorrect. A truer version would be: "Time is *LIFE*". The scarcest of all our resources is time. All other resources can be recovered, recycled, reused, or even replaced with substitutes. We can do none of these with time. We are given a fixed quantity each day, which will never vary, no matter how well or badly we use it. Men and women around the world feel that they simply do not have enough time to do all the things that they have or want to do. Consequently, people today feel pressured, overworked, fatigued, stressed and incapable of fulfilling all their responsibilities.

Whether expressed consciously or not, the ultimate goal of most human beings is happiness. Hence so much effort goes into acquiring material things, like cars, houses, and so on, because people associate having these things with happiness. Likewise, people sometimes feel that if they can just get caught up with their work, then they will be happy. But, even if we were miraculously to clear out all our outstanding tasks, we will at best only find a fleeting moment of happiness is at the end of these exertions.

Most people are so busy rushing back and forth that they seldom take the time to think seriously about *who* they are, and *why* they are doing what they are doing. They engage in frantic activity, instead of planned productivity. You will read this phrase several times in this book: "activity **is not** productivity". So, how can we break out of the activity cycle and set up a productivity cycle? How can we be more time productive and happier?

Dr. Steven R. Covey, in his book, "The 7 Habits of Highly Effective People" recommends that we set goals for ourselves. Our goals can fall under distinct categories, for example: Personal, Professional, Family and Community goals. But how can we prioritize among these? Many people seem to place professional goals on top of their list. Is this a fair and true reflection of your priorities? To find out if this is so, Covey then suggests that you imagine that you have six months to live. With this scenario, people generally realize that whatever quarrels they may have with other people are all petty in the long run, and they go on to reconcile with brothers, sisters, or friends where the relationships have deteriorated.

This indicates that most of our happiness in life will come from our personal relationships, with one expert suggesting that is as much as 85%. Our interactions with the people we care about provide our major source of pleasure and satisfaction. The other 15 percent comes from our accomplishments. Unfortunately, many people lose sight of what is truly important. They sacrifice their relationships to accomplish more in their careers. But a job can be only a minor source of the happiness we all seek with those closest to us. As Covey puts it, they climb the ladder of success just to realize, as they get to the top, that the ladder is placed against the **wrong wall!**

When setting your personal goals, it is important to give some serious thought to what you really value in life. When two goals appear to be in conflict, you prioritize based on your values. So, a key part of goal setting is to define and prioritize your values. If you believe and value one thing and yet find yourself doing another, you will cause yourself stress and unhappiness. Only when your values and your activities are coherent do you feel happy and at peace with yourself.

Knowing yourself means knowing what you really value, knowing what is important to you. A highly effective person decides what is right before he or she decides what is possible. Then he or she organizes his or her life to assure that everything is consistent with his or her true values. It is essential that you organize your life around yourself, your goals, and your values, rather than through inaction allow the external world to organize you around its demands. As the saying goes: "if you don't plan your life, someone else will!"

Regarding your work and family, continually ask yourself, "**What is the most valuable use of my time right now?**" Consider if what you are doing today will matter a week or a year from today. Sometimes, we become preoccupied with small things that are not important in the long run.

What is important in the long run is the quality of our home life and our happiness.

09

Our invisible backpacks which
harm our productivity

Henry Ford said, "If you believe you can, or if you believe you can´t, in both cases you are right."

What did he mean by this?

Canadian management and motivational specialist, Brian Tracy, talks about the often-invisible barriers which hold us back from achieving our true productive potential, exercising a vice-like influence. He refers to them as our "psychological backpacks". We carry them around and get so used to the sensation, we forget they are there.

To give an example of this phenomenon, let us use a fun exercise from the early 1980´s. Some of you may know it already, others will not, but whether you have seen it before or not, please go along with the flow for the purposes of this explanation.

Examine the 9 circles or dots, as shown below:

Even if you think you have seen the exercise before and know the solution, please take a few minutes to do it. Please DO NOT GOOGLE.

The exercise is this: take a pencil and join the nine dots together with only four continuous and straight lines. "Continuous lines" means that you do not lift your pen or pencil off the paper. If you draw a line going back on itself, it counts as 2 lines, not one.

The exercise should take 5 seconds, but normally only one person in a group of 20 will eventually guess the answer within 5 minutes. Sometimes, some people know that they've seen the exercise before, but have forgotten the solution. But whether they have seen the exercise before or not, it is more important to understand the underlying cause for the inability to see the solution quickly.

The reason why most people fail to see a solution is because they think (or believe) that it is necessary to stay within the confines of the nine dots, as if there were an imaginary box surrounding them. The solution consists in going outside the imaginary boundaries. Notice that these boundaries do not exist in the instruction to the exercise. The only place where the boundaries exist is in the mind of the person doing the exercise, and so it is what a person believes that limits him or her even though there is no basis for that belief.

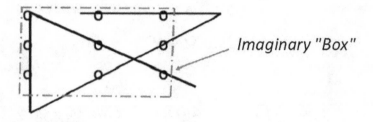

Imaginary "Box"

Some people do not see the solution because they think they must remain within the confines of the 9 dots, as if they imagine a "box" around the nine dots. Such a box does not exist in reality. It is a mental invention, a self-imposed imaginary rule. Only our imagination tells us to remain inside the imaginary box. Our imagination is so powerful, that it can hold us back, just as if it were a chain hanging around our necks.

Let us call this box, the "regular performance box". We will give the four walls of the box names, easy to remember using the acronym 'PIBO'. The letter **P** stands for **perceptions** and **paradigms**, the letter **I** stands for **interpretations**, **B** stands for **beliefs** and the **O** stands for **opinions**.

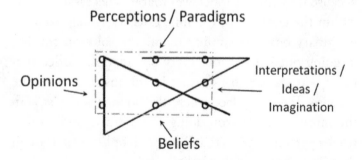

So, our perceptions, interpretations, beliefs, and opinions can hold us back just as if they were actual concrete walls around us. If we believe that we can't do something, even if that belief is untrue, the end result is that we won't be able to do that thing. And around these 4 walls, there is an even thicker wall called 'Fears'. In fact, these imaginary walls are so dangerous, precisely because we are not even aware that they are there, holding us back.

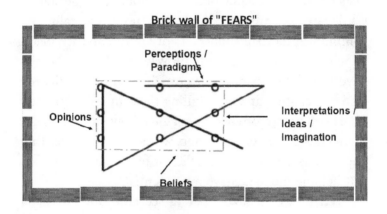

Henry Ford used the word, "think". All the components of the PIBO box are just different forms of thinking. To paraphrase his quote, whatever you perceive, interpret, believe, or hold a strong opinion on, becomes your reality.

Why should we hold ourselves back from experiencing our full potential because of some rules which we have unconsciously invented for ourselves, but which in reality do not exist? No one said that we could not go outside the box. Hence the phrase, "thinking outside the box".

You may say, "fun, interesting exercise, but so what? What are the implications of this in my everyday life?"

To leave the box of regular performance, we need to think beyond it, enter into another zone, first of uncertainty and then excellence.

We humans are so ready to fight to defend our beliefs, opinions, perceptions, or interpretations as if they were an integral part of our personality and our being. Indeed, these walls are so powerfully entrenched in our minds, that as human beings, we are the only animals on Earth which kill our own kind because the other person does not share the same beliefs. Catholics or Protestants, Christians or atheists, Arabs or Jews, capitalist or communist, football supporters of United or City, black or white, are only some of the ways we human beings have found to separate ourselves into groups and thus justify alienating and even killing those in other groups.

If beliefs are often unconscious, how can we make them conscious? As a first step, we can ask ourselves this question: is this particular belief or fear inhibiting me or is it helping me to achieve my potential?

When we realize that a certain and perhaps unconscious belief limits us (such as, *"I am not capable of generating great ideas"*), then we make a great stride forward. We have a power that other animals do not. We can choose our beliefs CONSCIOUSLY. We can consciously CHOOSE to replace any negative belief with another more positive and powerful one, such as:

'*I can generate spectacular ideas*', or
'*I am the expert in my area*', or
'*Management respects and values my opinions*',
and so on.

"Thinking out of the box" implies a conscious effort to change beliefs, opinions, interpretations, and thoughts as a route to discovering creative solutions to problems. Many times, the real problem is not the problem itself, but the invisible backpack of unconscious beliefs with which we are operating. So, before frantically rushing headlong into tackling a problem, take some time out in order to examine the set of beliefs and assumptions, which you bring to the problem. Write them down. Challenge them. Often, by challenging and changing these beliefs and assumptions, a simple "out of the box" solution pops up as if by magic.

10

The Only Constant is Change

You can break human laws and get away with it. In fact, thousands of criminals count on it! But unlike human laws, the laws of Nature have an impersonal and universal characteristic: no matter how much we try to resist, or protest that nature is unfair, we cannot break these laws. For example, please try now to break the Law of Gravity. If you decide to try, and break your legs, do not say that nature is cruel: the law is universal and applies equally to all, saints and sinners alike.

Another universal characteristic of nature is that it is always changing. The very atoms of which you are composed are vibrating at unimaginable speeds, imperceptibly and constantly changing your body, whether you like it or not. A rock which appears inanimate is in fact teeming with swarming electrons at a sub-microscopic level.

"Okay," you may say, "at a microscopic level, I accept that we are in constant movement, but at our level of magnitude, change is very slow and gradual."

Is this just a misleading perception, or reality? If it were the second alternative, what then is the reality that we are not perceiving, that our senses do not register? At this very moment, all of us are changing our position in the universe at a speed of almost 30 kilometers per second! How can this be so? We are all aboard a spaceship called "Planet Earth", which travels 942 million kilometers each year as it orbits our Sun. Work out the math for yourself. [*3]

You will eventually come to the conclusion that the only constant in the Universe is change. Nothing is ever totally at rest (except at absolute zero temperature, where there is a total absence of energy!) So, applying this law of nature to ourselves and to our companies, we can see that whenever we resist change or try to slow it down, we are in effect trying to alter a Law of Nature, and as such, it won't end well for us.

There is a harmful belief which seeds destruction in thousands of companies. This is the belief that we are already working the best we can in the best possible way, or what we are doing is good enough. This unconscious belief implicitly says is that we have already reached perfection, that there is no longer a need for change. This is a "Tombstone Belief" because it kills companies. It runs

---

[*3] Distance from the Earth to the Sun = 150 million kilometers

Distance travelled by the Earth around the Sun in a year = 942 million kilometers

Speed of the Earth = 942.000.000 kilometers / 365 days / 24 hours / 60 minutes / 60 seconds = 29.9 kilometers / second

against the very fabric of nature. Nature is unforgiving: she eventually kills off those who try to break her laws.

When we realize that we have a certain, perhaps unconscious belief that limits us (such as, "I am not capable of generating great ideas"), we have made a great stride forward. We can consciously CHOOSE to replace this negative belief with another more positive and powerful one. We can CHOOSE to re-program ourselves with a more powerful set of beliefs. Change our beliefs, and we change our reality.

The former CEO of General Electric, Jack Welch, summed it up: "If the rate of change outside your organization is greater than the rate of change within your organization, then the end of your company is already in sight."

11

Changing behaviors to Improve your Personal Performance

C hildren learn quickly: they naturally adopt new behaviors and new ways of looking at the world. But we adults become set in our ways, we find it more difficult to change our behavior and our beliefs. We seem to operate with the underlying assumptions or beliefs, *"that is just the way I am, you cannot expect me to change at my time in life"*, or *"a leopard never changes its spots"*, or *"you can't teach an old dog new tricks"*. These are typical ATTITUDES (from the SABRe model in Chapter 1), and debilitating beliefs (see Chapter 7). The good news is that they are all totally **untrue**.

We have already mentioned that doing the same thing repeatedly and expecting different results leads nowhere.

We seek to generate a different result: a significant improvement in our personal productivity through changing our behavior. Whether we are talking about adults or children, it is useful to consider that behavior change occurs in three stages:

(1) COMPLIANCE,
(2) UNDERSTANDING, and
(3) USAGE.

To illustrate each of these stages, let's use the analogy of learning to drive a car. Take a trip back in time to when you were learning to drive. Imagine being seated for the first time behind the steering wheel. In the passenger seat is your driving instructor, a parent, relative or a qualified instructor from a driving school. This person gives you detailed step-by-step instructions: he tells you to start the engine, check your mirrors, put the car into first gear and so on. As a student wanting to learn, you comply exactly with what he tells you to do. Probably you do not know how a car works, nor probably do you much care; your keenest wish is simply to learn to drive, so you do exactly what he says.

In short, you COMPLY.

This is the first stage in the process of adult learning: COMPLIANCE.

After a while of just doing what your instructor requests you to do, you start to UNDERSTAND a bit of what's going on. You understand that when you press down on the gas pedal, but you haven't released the handbrake, you stall the engine. You understand this because you have done it several times -- experience teaches you. Imagine this: instead of allowing you to learn from experience, your instructor tells you that you would stall the car while trying to move off with the handbrake still on. Probably his words would go in one ear and straight out the other -- in a few moments, you would probably forget what he had told you. Worse still, imagine just reading it, without even listening to the words of an instructor. You will understand the words intellectually, but you will never really understand in your body what stalling an engine feels like. You will forget the words you read within 5 minutes. However, when you learn from experience, when you incorporate the learning (*"incorporate"* means *"bring into the body"*) you remember it more easily and forever.

You are now in the second stage of adult learning -- UNDERSTANDING. You understand the cause - effect nature of things: cause = changing gears too quickly; effect = stalling engine. You continue to practice, getting better all the time.

When you arrive at a deep understanding, you are now ready to use your knowledge to drive yourself without the instructor at your side. You observe effects (a drop in speed going uphill); you analyze the causes (not changing gear) and now you take corrective action (you change down gear and press on the gas pedal).

Now you are in the final stage: **USAGE.**

This car analogy is quite simple and a fair reflection of what happens when adopting a new behavior. However, there are some key differences between the car analogy and many other work-place situations. These differences can lead to people giving up at the first stage: **compliance.**

A child will fall off his or her bicycle many times while attempting to learn the behaviors necessary for riding the bike, and willingly gets back on the bike. The child is SELF-MOTIVATED to learn. He or she will suffer the pains of falling, and the embarrassing moments, because he WANTS TO LEARN. But adults often stumble at the first obstacle, and quit the learning process at the first stage, which is compliance. The reasons are fear, over-confidence, not understanding the process, embarrassment; all of which are perceived as public blows to the ego. Only by becoming aware of the process, can you overcome these obstacles. The key realizations are awareness and competency.

There is another useful way of looking at adult learning of any new activity. These are the four phases of being:

-- unconsciously incompetent.
-- *consciously* incompetent.
-- *consciously* competent.
-- unconsciously competent.

LEVEL OF COMPETENCE

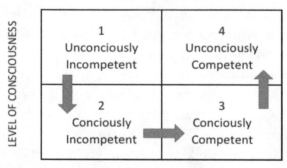

At the start of any new behavior, whether it be riding a bike or learning yoga or karate or how to read a balance sheet or an architectural drawing, we are **unaware** of how little we know.

We see other people riding on their bikes, and we think it looks easy to do. We think that we can also do it easily; and all this before we ever go near a bike. We have no idea of the great surprise in store for us when we get on a bike for the first time -- falling off, scraping knees, chafed elbows, and the rest of it. Not only did we not know how to ride a bike, but we were also blissfully unaware of our ignorance.

We are unaware of our incompetence: we are **unconsciously incompetent.**

The same phenomenon exists at the start of any new behavior; we get the impression that it looks all too easy. Are we in for a surprise!

Returning to the bike analogy, let us say someone gives us our first bike. Excitedly we get on. That takes some working out. Do you swing a leg over from the side or back ways? Once on, the seat feels uncomfortable and hard. Is it meant to feel like that? We push off, and immediately start wobbling from side to side. The swings and wobbles get bigger and bigger, and quick as a flash, we have experienced our very first fall off a bike.

We have just learned the hard way that we cannot ride a bike. Now we KNOW: there is absolutely no doubt in our minds. We have just become conscious of our incompetence.

We are **consciously incompetent.**

A similar thing happens when trying any new system or behavior. Because we have seen other people do it, and make it look easy, when we fail at our first attempt, we think that others will be looking at us, judging us as incompetent or stupid. So, what happens then? Pride comes into the picture. Instead of realizing that all we are experiencing is a normal healthy process with regard to learning, we try to defend ourselves from appearing stupid, by criticizing the system or behavior in question, looking for weaknesses, discrediting it, and trying to avoid using it. It's like saying: "I don't like that bike -- it's red, and blue is my favorite color." Or "the seat is too hard and too high": or "the gears are too stiff" or "it's too much work pedaling -- maybe I should have a motor bike instead."

The consciously incompetent phase is the most dangerous for adults, as this is where people tend to give up.

Fortunately, it does not have to be like this. Once people have had an explanation of how adult learning works, and once they understand that they are simply passing through the very normal process, their resistance fades away. This requires a change of mindset, an acceptance of the clumsiness and awkwardness as part and parcel of the new learning experience.

With further practice, the adult continues to get better at the new behavior. As the person is concentrating on what he/she is doing, now the person reaches the phase of being **consciously competent.** In addition, with perseverance, the person continually gets better, and one day can behave in the new manner without any concentration or conscious effort. In the bike analogy, this person can ride the bike without even thinking about it. He or she has become **unconsciously competent.**

Whenever you learn a new process or method, please be patient and loving with yourself. Do this by recognizing where you are on the adult learning scale and accepting it as a natural part of the growth process.

12

Improving quality of life with the
Pareto Effect (the 80/20 rule)

I magine a Monday morning, it is 8:30am, and you
arrive at your office.

As you start your working day, sipping your morning
coffee, you see that you have 30 items on your To-Do
list. No problem, you think, I'll whip all these monkeys
into shape before the end of the week! Shakespeare said
something about "the best laid plans of mice and men",
and if to prove the point, just as you settle down to tackling
the first item on your list, your boss appears at your office
door. There is a crisis in one of the Regional Offices, and
you are being sent there to sort it out. He hands you your
air ticket for that afternoon and tells you to expect to be
there for at least a week. You inwardly groan, "what about
this stack of things I've got to get done before the end of
the week?", and you know that it would be a painful but
pointless exercise to mention this to your boss. You can
almost hear his retort of "well, you're a manager, aren't
you? Manage it!" So, how are you going to manage it? As
an approach, fortunately, we have the benefit of the work

done by a 19th Century Italian mathematician named Alfredo Pareto. This is what Pareto discovered.

In most fields of human activity and nature, we find that 80% of the effects usually result from only 20% of the causes. Let's look at some examples.

In your living room, you will observe that 80% of the wear of the carpet occurs over only 20% of its area.

At a social meeting, typically 20% of the invitees will tell 80% of the jokes.

In political geography, it is not uncommon for 80% of the population of a country to live in only 20% of the available land area.

In football, 80% of the goals are scored by only 20% of the players. Also, over the whole league, 80% of the goals are scored by only 20% of the teams.

In social economy, 80% of the wealth of the world is in the hands of 20% of the population.

In sales, 80% of the income is generated by 20% of the sales force. Typically, only 20% of a company's products will represent 80% of its inventories.

This phenomenon is often called the "Pareto Effect", and it should be no surprise to know that it is also referred to as the "80-20 rule".

Now, if we look at how we can apply this guideline to the productive use of your (a typical manager's) time, you can say something like, "80% of the positive impacts that I achieve usually come from only 20% of my actions." You remember that a key concept in productivity measurement is the idea of "value added to the client" and its opposite, "Muda". This implies that of the 30 items on your "To-Do List", typically only 6 will really add value. These are therefore the best bets. So, faced with only a few hours before catching the plane, you ask yourself, "what is the most important thing I can do now, what thing will add most value, assuming that it is the only thing I have got time to do?" You then dedicate yourself to completing that task. If you finish it and still have some time remaining, you repeat the question, and so on until the top six are done. And even if they are not, you can still leave for the airport in the knowledge that although you did not do everything that you had planned to do, those things that you did complete were precisely those that add greatest value to your company and / or to your clients.

13

Improving Executive Productivity with less stress

If you ask a group of senior executives to estimate how productive they are, they will usually say between 80%, 90% and some even >100%. Most executives are blissfully unaware that they are totally mistaken. When estimating their personal productivity, most executives end up estimating their *ACTIVITY* levels.

Let us see how this works. Assume a typical executive works an 11-hour day. Out of these 11 hours, he sees that he has been actively involved doing things for about 10 hours. Therefore, he says, "my productivity is equal to:

$$\frac{10 \text{ hours spent doing stuff}}{11 \text{ hours spent at work}} \quad = \quad 91\% \text{ productivity}"$$

Peter Drucker, a management guru, once said, "what you measure, you get!" Using the above measure, the more stressed out an executive is, and the longer hours he works, apparently the better! Unfortunately, this measure is not only misleading, but also dangerous for his health, and that of his Company! What is he doing wrong, then?

Well, it is not so much a case of DOING anything wrong, it is more a case of laboring under a wrong perception or paradigm. When working as performance coaches with senior executives, we often find something like the following:

How the executive perceives his performance:			*How it actually is:*		
$\dfrac{\text{hours in activity}}{\text{hours at work}}$	=	$\dfrac{10}{11}$	$\dfrac{\text{hours ADDING VALUE}}{\text{hours at work}}$	=	$\dfrac{1}{11}$
=	**91% *ACTIVE***		=	**9% *PRODUCTIVE***	

Most executives are at first deeply shocked when they see that their true productivity is often less than 10%! Even though their instinct had told them something was probably wrong when they thought they were working at a 91% activity levels, it takes some time to grasp the fact that the percentage of their time actually spent on real value-adding activities is so low. At this point, we tell them that rather than consider this as bad news, why not view it as good news? Because it means that they can double their effectiveness, while working less, thus improving the quality of their lives, and having more time to spend with their families. This is how:

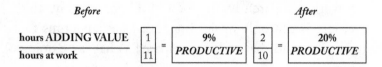

Notice that while the executive's hours at work have dropped from 11 to 10, his effectiveness has more than doubled. In addition to increasing his effectiveness, this executive has one hour extra each day to spend with his family, to practice a sport, or to further his education. And because he is less stressed, his performance at work will further improve in the longer term.

14

The 5 Personal Productivity
Filters and using your subconscious

In this Chapter, we make use of some of the common-sense ideas presented in previous chapters, to help you use the 1,440 minutes you get each day to your best effect.

Write out your "To Do List", forget it, then let your subconscious get to work.

Most people write out their "To Do Lists" at the start of their working days. Change that. Instead, at the **_end_** of each working day, write everything down on your "To-Do List", examine it through the **5 Personal Productivity Filters**.

They say "time is money". More important than that, your time is your LIFE. Just because something is on your To-Do List, does not automatically mean that you have to do it. You can still decide to scrub it.

Examine each item on your To-Do List and check its agreement with the following 5 Personal Productivity Filters. If it fails, scrub it! Scrub it!

Filter No. 1: Your Values.

Work only on those things that are consistent with your values, eliminating those that do not. Being unfaithful to your own values has many consequences on a personal and professional level, not least a reduction in your personal productivity. A poor example which should never happen: your boss asks you to tell a white lie to a client over a telephone call you have to make. If one of your values is HONESTY; scrub it!

Filter No. 2: Value-Added.

Ask yourself whether the action adds value to your client or the product or service you provide for your client. Also ask yourself if the proposed action adds value to the realization of your personal goals and dreams. If not: scrub it!

Filter No. 3: Law of the Harvest.

Every effect has a cause, every action has a reaction. If your action is a seed, ask yourself what crop you will reap by doing this action. Then, look at the other side of the coin. Ask yourself what crop you will reap by NOT doing this action. These questions help you to see which actions have higher value-added.

Filter No. 4: Use the Pareto Effect.

20% of what you do gives 80% of your results. Ask yourself whether each action is among the 20% that creates the most value-added and prioritize them accordingly. *REFER TO CHAPTER 12.*

Filter No. 5: Keep Clear in mind the difference between Urgent and Important.

Important activities often fall by the wayside, victims to the urgent. Unexpected phone calls or visitors appear urgent, but perhaps the consequences of dealing (or not dealing) with them may not be that important. Urgent demands often cause you to deviate from what is important. If your Urgent is also important, then do it straight away.

Use your subconscious: first activation

After writing out your list and passing it through the five filters, visualize yourself in your mind's eye doing and completing what you need to do. This motivates your subconscious towards completing actions. Say, for example, that you want to close a deal in a meeting tomorrow. Visualize yourself with a smile giving your client a warm handshake to seal the agreement at the end of the meeting.

Use your subconscious: second activation

Now........*forget about it! Put it out of your thoughts.* Go home, be totally conscious of your "here and now", see a movie, be with friends, whatever. During the night while you sleep, your subconscious (your free super-computer) will carry on working on your goals. And when you wake up, you will feel your engine already tuned up for the day ahead.

Planning goes a long way in helping you achieve your goals. There is no short cut for planning. Not planning is a decision, just as planning is.

Failing to Plan is Planning to Fail.

15

The biggest Muda of all

The Japanese word, Muda, describes everything happening within a company which fails to add value to the product or service for the client. Some everyday examples include duplication, waiting time, excess inventories, wastage of materials, scrap, rework, wastage of energy, unnecessary movement, unnecessary stress or effort, excessive distances covered, 90% of memos written and read, bureaucracy, time wasted in meetings, wasted spaces, lost sales, overproduction, etc.

But all of these are just symptoms. The underlying cause of all of these is, in my view, the greatest Muda of all, and the one still waiting to be tackled with fierce honesty in organizations.

What is this great beast, this mother of all Mudas?

In a nutshell, it is everything which deviates from what trial lawyers call, "the truth, the whole truth, and nothing but the truth."

Does this sound like a gross exaggeration?

Imagine you are a fly on the wall of a weekly management meeting, in a typical company, anywhere.

Imagine you can hear the innermost thoughts of the participants when their thoughts do not coincide with their words.

The Sales Manager says: "our sales are down again, because we are still waiting for the new computerized customer tracking system, and Production only fulfilled 67% of our orders". He thinks, *"Sales are really down because the competition is cheaper, but this computer system is 6 months overdue, and I need it. It would have helped me focus more on the marketplace. So, I am not going to let these Systems guys off the hook! And Production never does better than 67% of their program anyway! If I were the General Manager, I would sort this lot out! I cannot understand why he does not see through this bull."*

The IT Manager says, "our supplier is behind schedule and is putting extra resources onto the project, at obviously no extra cost for us, and the system will be ready by next month", but thinks, *"if you guys had been involved in the beginning as you promised, you wouldn't have wasted months each time you constantly changed your minds about what you want from the system. Perhaps if you paid for the system yourself out of your own budget, you would have shown more commitment."*

The Production Manager says, "True, we did only fulfill 67% of orders, but Sales only told us what they want on the 20th, when they were supposed to inform us on the 12th," and thinks *"those guys in sales are so badly organized they couldn't organize a drinking session in a brewery. I'm sorry, buddy, but YOUR lack of planning does not constitute MY crisis!"*

The General Manager says, "Guys, we can only resolve this by acting together as a team," and thinks, *"the*

Sales Manager is very chummy with the President, went to the same school, and I reckon that he is trying to make us all look bad so that he can line himself up for promotion into my job. I can't wait until we get the new computer system online and we can blow that excuse of his out of the water, then I can fire HIM!"

Here we have a lack of honesty, and zero confidence in the team. Imagine a football team trying to win a league with such a spirit among the team players! Impossible!

In this imaginary scenario, the greatest Muda is caused by the lack of honesty and confidence in the members of the Top Management Team. Some of the consequences of this are:

❖ The function of each Manger *should be* to provide maximum value to the service or product that they deliver to their clients. But we see in that weekly management meeting that each of the top 4 executives has a hidden agenda, and customer value added does not even register on the group radar.

❖ The hidden agenda of the Sales Manager is to discredit his peers and set himself up for a promotion, using his close friendship with the President.

❖ The hidden agenda of the IT Manager is to avoid responsibility for the delayed implementation of a new computer system, blaming first the supplier, and as a back-up, the Sales Dept for their constant changes to requirements.

❖ The hidden agenda of the Production Manager is to merely follow established procedures because he perceives that his colleagues in Sales are badly organized, and he sees this as the best way to pressurize them into getting their act together, while protecting his own position.

❖ And the General Manager also has a hidden agenda. He sees that the Sales Director meets socially with his President, and suspects machinations to remove him and replace him with the Sales Manager. He believes that the drop in sales has little to do with the availability or not of the new computer system and is pressurizing the IT Manager to get the new system running so that he can eliminate the Sales Manager's excuse for dropping sales and then fire him!

Not one of those four hidden intentions adds value to the service or product that the company provides for its clients. Some people use the term "political in-fighting" to describe this environment. Nobody appears to be *primarily* concerned about WHY the sales are dropping. The hidden intentions lead to the top 4 executives generating 100% Muda, a very expensive meeting for the company.

Each of these four executives will propagate further Muda in the organization through their interactions with their subordinates and close colleagues, some of whom may even be actively involved in pursuing the hidden objective of their immediate boss, rather than the overall company objective.

Napoleon Hill, in his book, "Think and Grow Rich", speaks of the advice given to him by Andrew Carnegie, at that time the world's richest man. Carnegie told him about the "Mastermind" principle. When two or more people get together in a spirit of harmony in pursuit of a common objective, a powerful and positive energy is created between them, as if a Mastermind were at work. By the same token, when negative feelings exist between team members, the Mastermind energy created between them is even more destructive.

This company is sick. The symptoms of its sickness are political infighting, and a culture of protecting one's own interests. The Company neglects its clients and deteriorates. If this is allowed to persist, there is only one future for the company: bankruptcy.

How do you tackle this corporate sickness?

What follows will seem to you so deceptively easy, that many people will consider it too simple and superficial. And that may be why you chose to pass this over and fail to implement it. Sometimes there is *nothing harder to do than that which is absolutely right.*

The top person in a company, the President / Chairman / CEO, has one primordial responsibility. This is to define CONSCIOUSLY the values by which the organization is to live, to continuously communicate these values, <u>to exemplify those values</u> **<u>by his or her own behavior.</u>** This is the most effective way to promote adherence to those values by all employees within the organization. This means being totally faithful on a personal level to these consciously elected values. Failure to define one's values means that one ends up working to a set of arbitrary or random values, which may or may not be those best suited for the long-term success and survival of the business. Just like a garden, if we do not consciously plant the flowers we want, weeds WILL come in and take over!

Through leading by example, being the living embodiment of the Company's values, the CEO exercises the *OPTIMUM PRODUCTIVITY CONTROL SYSTEM*. Because the underlying values of the organization are so clearly defined and lived, the CEO can be reasonably sure that at any one moment in time, while he may not know what a particular manager is doing, he can be pretty certain that whatever it is, most of the time it is in agreement with the organization's basic values.

If someone is found to have acted against those values, providing top management have done enough to communicate and demonstrate those values, then that person should be promptly ejected from the organization.

An organization that has had a clear set of values is IBM. Thomas Watson Jr., son of the founder, in his book of 1963 called "A Business and its Beliefs", wrote that the values that his father built into the organization were:

- Respect for the individual
- Major attention to service
- Superiority in all things.

When IBM deviated from these values, in the mid 80´s, it ran into problems and almost went under. It confused "Superiority in all things" as meaning THEY were superior, not their products or services. This complacency allowed two upstarts, Apple and Microsoft, to leapfrog them.

Miele, the German top-market white goods manufacturer, lives its values, expressed as "Immer

Besser". This means, "always better", always seeking improvement. Like the Japanese word, "Kaizen", which means "continuous improvement"? Steve Jobs once commented that the device he most admired outside of Apple was a Miele washing machine.

Another example of an organization with clearly expressed values may even be a country. The constitution of the United States reflects the values of the founding fathers. "We, the people..."

What are your organization's values? Are they consciously chosen and lived out, or happenstance?

16

How incorrect performance measures
can harm customer service

As performance improvement facilitators, we occasionally see a manager taking a decision "because it will increase our productivity". Sometimes, an action taken to increase productivity may have the unwanted side effect of damaging customer service. For example, the manager may say something like: "I must produce Alpha, Beta, Gamma, Delta and Epsilon in more or less regular quantities each month. But if I produce five lots of Alpha in month 1, five lots of Beta in month 2, etcetera, I will save 4 setup times per month and will therefore be much more productive. Good idea, yes?"

When we say: "No, it is not a good idea", the manager is usually surprised. "I thought you would be pleased that I am improving productivity", he protests.

Sometimes (no, almost always!), it is difficult to change a paradigm. When we explain that customer service is more important than his productivity indicator (at this stage, it is still too early in his paradigm change to tell him that he is very probably measuring the wrong thing), you can see the veins throb on his forehead. We ask: "But what happens to those customers waiting for products Beta, Gamma, Delta, and Epsilon at the end of month 1? They wait, and wait, and eventually buy the competitor's (sometimes inferior) product."

Productivity should never come at the expense of customer service. If it does, it is because we are measuring productivity incorrectly.

If you are asked to measure productivity in a company which allows its managers to decide what to do without consideration of what their customers want and when they want it, you should give zero credit to everything produced which does not meet a customer's specific need. So, in the case above, if customers were asking for one lot each of products Alpha, Beta, Gamma, Delta and Epsilon, by producing only product Alpha, our productivity will be **at best only 20%.**

A service industry example: imagine that an IT department has five projects to add value to its customers, via improving its products or services, and eight projects for other areas in the company, such as Human Resources, Finance, etcetera. In a certain week, the manager dedicates all his resources to work exclusively on the eight internal projects, thinking (his paradigm) that it is important to maintain optimum relations with his colleagues. It cannot be shown that these internal projects will enhance customer service. Therefore, you should classify the departmental productivity as zero. If we were to measure the activity level within the department, we would probably find that the department is 80% active in carrying out its activities. So, how can we be 80% active, but 0% productive? Because activity is not necessarily productivity. Working to add customer value is productive work. Every other activity, however strenuous, hard, intense, and stressful it may be, as it fails to add value, gives a zero contribution to productivity.

How many customer-irrelevant activities are happening right now in your organization?

Find the answer to that question and you are on the trail to finding the goldmine in your Company.

17

How you treat your people affects customer service

We often hear phrases like: "our people are our greatest assets." Look at the Balance Sheet of a typical company. Where do these "greatest assets" appear?

Other assets, like buildings, machines, equipment, etc., are recognized on the Balance Sheet, and are given a depreciation over time. A car may be depreciated in 5 years, a building in 30, for example.

The human asset is different: not only does it not appear as such on the balance sheet, but also it does not depreciate; it **appreciates** in value over time. An employee normally acquires experience, knowledge, and wisdom with time, making him or her MORE VALUABLE to the Company.

Even now in the 21st Century, many managers still seem to believe that their main purpose is to maximize the profits of their organization. To achieve this, they can deploy the various resources at their disposal. The five Ms:

Men----Machines----Materials-----Money----Management.

Under this way of looking at things (this paradigm), subordinates are considered on par with tools or equipment, just another means that the manager can use to achieve his ends: "the end justifies the means" is the common wisdom. This is reflected by the fact that many companies' Mission Statements usually emphasize shareholder returns and superior customer attention. Little mention is made of the value of the employees in the organization.

This type of thinking dehumanizes us. As we already discussed, a human is made up of three complementary parts: body, mind, heart. Every company focuses on how to get the most efficiency out of a person's physical movements, whether it might be inserting components into a machine, typing letters on a keyboard, processing documents, or making telephone calls, etcetera. With bible-thick tomes of procedures and guidelines, the employee is told exactly what he or she must do in any foreseen circumstance. If something comes out of the ordinary, heaven forbid that he should use his initiative! The procedure says that the employee must go and find the supervisor. Thus, he or she is inhibited from using the second part, his or her brain. And fear or indifference keeps an employee from tapping into passion, spirit, or soul. This is the part most difficult to define but is by far the most powerful component of a human. A successful entrepreneur operates almost entirely on his heart / passion / soul...... can you imagine anyone who has been wildly successful without being deeply passionate about what he or she does?

If we assign equal weighting to these three human parts, this means that as companies tend to focus almost exclusively on the first, we are at best using only 33% of the power of our employees. What would happen if we were to change our paradigm? Instead of saying, "The customer comes first", why not say, "we place our employees first". This is the paradigm in the Virgin Group, founded by Richard Branson.

This alternative paradigm states that, by making our priority an active and conscious decision to foster the personal, professional, financial, and even spiritual growth of our employees, they will naturally and automatically seek to deliver outstanding customer service. If we treat our employees excellently, the chances are that they in turn will treat the customers likewise.

A challenge remains: how do we incorporate our human assets onto the balance sheet?

If a key employee left, how much would it cost the company to replace her?

18

How values affect corporate behavior

Generally Accepted Accountancy Principles (GAAP) allow companies to depreciate the cost of a purchased asset, like a vehicle or a machine, over its useful life, say 3 to 5 years.

There is a set of intangible assets, which have a direct bearing on the long-term profitability of the company and yet not considered within GAAP. These are the declared **_and lived_** corporate values or Principles. Values (such as love, kindness, honesty) are timeless, which infers that their financial value should not vary over time.

Once you consciously decide on a set of values, it is also necessary to prioritize them. This facilitates decision-making whenever an event appears to cause a conflict of values.

Here is an example. Three companies in the same industry with the same product have the same set of values, but ranked differently, as shown below:

Company X	Company Y	Company Z
Shareholder returns	Customer Service	Integrity
Customer Service	Community	Quality
Quality	Integrity	Shareholder returns
Community	Shareholder returns	Customer Service
Integrity	Quality	Community

Imagine that they each suddenly face the same scenario. A defect has been found in the star product, possibly affecting one in a million of the units sold, and which could possibly cause an accident to the user.

The management teams in each company explore 3 alternative courses of action. They are:

Action A. *Recall all products.* This would have a cost of $50 million but would send a strong message to the customers that the company places them first.

Action B. *Do nothing.* This would have no initial cost, but the managers recognize that were there to be an accident, they would end up paying up to $20 million in legal settlements, with consequent loss of image. But the odds are in their favor.

Action C. *Inform all customers of defective units with warning signs.* This would have a cost of $10 million, as managers expect that up to 5% of the customers would approach them for a checkup. The managers decide to do it anyway, using the occasion to let customers know about the exciting new product lines.

Probably Company X, trying to maximize profits, would go for action B. Possibly Company Y, with its emphasis on customer service would adopt action A. And perhaps Company Z, where integrity is the overriding value, would seek to adopt action C.

The purpose of this example is to create awareness of the importance of the process of consciously selecting a set of values and their rank. If you do not consciously plant the flowers you want in your garden, you will not get a barren garden, but a set of random weeds. As nature abhors a vacuum, human nature abhors an absence of declared values.

One day perhaps we will see audit companies including a statement in the audited accounts regarding the values (moral, not financial) of the client company they audit. *"Company A has a clear mission of increasing shareholder value. This is the number one value and key to advancement throughout the organization. However, we are concerned that we find no reference to ethical principles or honesty in the company's mission statement, and we feel that employees will be encouraged to consider that it is acceptable to allow some small dishonesty, PROVIDED OF COURSE THAT NO ONE SHOULD EVER FIND OUT, to secure a profit advantage. Consequently, we have advised a downgrading of the shareholder equity to reflect this weakness."*

Unlikely? Perhaps one day, GAAP will include some external and subjective-objective assessment of the long-term viability of a company because of the values practiced within.

Until then, when you are considering working for Company X, Y or Z, you are now aware that the declared values help you determine whether the company is a good cultural fit for you, considering your goals and objectives.

In your interviews, ask for examples of specific behaviors which show how the values are being practiced daily in the company.

19

Improving performance through changing attitudes

S o how do you go about generating a significant performance improvement?

An obvious way is to purchase more modern and faster equipment: technological investment. A broken-down machine, beyond hope of repair, obviously needs replacement.

Sometimes, even when an old technology still works adequately, it is better to pay the cost for a new technology. A manufacturer who insisted on maintaining his line of carburetors at all costs *("if it ain't broke, why fix it?")* went out of business in just a few years, when electronic fuel injectors came to market, which were much more fuel-efficient than carburetors.

What can you do when everyone has acquired a new technology? Everyone has email, internet, intranet, conference call facilities, on-line management control systems, personal digital assistants, AI software, etc. What else can you do to generate a competitive advantage?

One path is "let our people be our competitive advantage". Even at the start of the 21st Century, too many companies are still using only a fraction of the productive potential of their people. Here is an oversimplified example to illustrate the point. If a company employs a person to perform only certain physical movements (answer this telephone, pack those boxes, mind this machine, deliver these packages, etc...), then that company is only using at best 33% of the capabilities of the employee. A human being is made up of a body, a brain, and a third component which is more difficult to put into words, but which may be described collectively as heart, passion, soul or spirit. How many companies *CONSCIOUSLY* try to tap into all three of these components? Not many.

The body working with the brain coupled with the power of passion / heart / spirit can truly produce wonderful productive results for the company.

So, how do you tap into this power?

Change the attitudes / paradigms of management and supervision.

The normal paradigm of a manager is that his first responsibility is to maximize profits. To that end, the employees are like tools or equipment at his disposal to get the job done.

We can consciously adopt another paradigm, best illustrated in the following Chinese proverb:

If you want one year of prosperity; grow wheat
If you want ten years of prosperity; grow trees
If you want 100 years of prosperity; grow people.

Under this paradigm, the foremost responsibility and duty of each manager or supervisor is to help each subordinate to develop his or her abilities to the maximum. As the employees grow, the company will also grow as a natural by-product.

You can add strength to this attitude / paradigm change by accompanying it with a system tool:

Here is a suggestion. Include as part of a manager's or supervisor's performance evaluation system, a measure of how well they have encouraged their subordinates' growth each year. For example: how many improvement ideas have you received from your employees and how many have you implemented with them?

What you measure, improves. See Chapter 27 for more on this topic.

20

Forming a High-Performance Team

"Be the change you want to see in the world".

Mahatma Gandhi

A senior manager once confided to us: "there seems to be a gap between what our declared values say, and what we actually do in practice. How can we change this?".

We all know what happens when change is imposed from outside or on high. People view this kind of change as repression. We resist the change, consciously or unconsciously, and the change will sooner or later be rejected. The repressive communist regimes of the former USSR imploded in 1989, creating a dozen independent countries. The repressive regimes in Cuba and Venezuela will undoubtedly collapse in time.

Extrapolating this lesson to a High-Performance Team (HPT), it is clear that dictating from on high, "managing from the throne", and imposing on team members will not work. The spirit of an HPT must spring from the hearts of its members.

Can a Company act as one large team? Intuition tells us that it is almost impossible for several hundred people to work effectively in unison. In practice, a company is more like a grouping of small teams, where some people belong to more than one team. The same principle applies to this grouping of teams as with a human being: change must come from within. The implication for a company is that the groups of teams mirror the leadership of a central, or Core Team.

Consider the word "core". In English, we use the word when talking about an apple core, or the core of the Earth. In French, "coeur". In Spanish, "corazón". Both these words translate back into English as "heart". This is a more accurate way of looking at the issue: the Core Team in a Company is the heart of the company. This is the team that sets the value base and the spiritual direction of the Company. As Jesus said, "As a man thinketh in his heart, so is he"; the Core Team is charged with the responsibility for *being* the change which must be produced within a company. Leadership must be through BEHAVIOR, not words.

Many managers believe that effective team building leads to greater productivity and a healthier bottom line. Then why are there so many management teams functioning at half steam? Here we explore some common fallacies about team building, and what to do about them.

A team is a group of individuals working together for a common purpose. On the surface, you could think that the greater the qualities of the individuals making up the team, then the greater is the quality of the team. But, when we look at examples from sport, often we see that a team with less talent or skill can win the trophy because of its greater spirit, passion, and commitment. For example, Real Madrid, the Spanish soccer "Galacticos", are sometimes beaten by teams of lesser quality players.

Nowadays, most companies have clearly expressed Visions, Missions and Values, but they still perceive that their teams operate ineffectively.

Why the disconnect between the declared Mission and the observed behavior? Mission statements are dictated from above, with top management expecting that everybody will miraculously work in the desired way. One reason for the disconnect is that people do not see a direct relation with the Company's mission to their everyday activities.

High-performance Teams display BEHAVIORS consistent with the Mission and values. So, how do we form a Highly Productive Teams?

The process starts with the top management of the company, which becomes the CORE TEAM. Once the Core Team is performing / behaving as it should, each manager can use the same process to develop Area Teams with his or her subordinates, with goals and values coherent with the Core.

Regardless of whether we are talking about a CORE or an AREA Team, the team building process is:

FORM → STORM → NORM → PERFORM

A team starts as a group of isolated people who just happen to work in the same area towards the same ends. This is how teams typically FORM. By chance.

To start becoming a Highly Productive team, we brainstorm our own goals or Mission, obviously coherent with the overall Company's. This is the STORM phase.

Then we need to decide HOW we will achieve these goals, in other words what are the ground rules to which we will work. In this phase, we will agree what our underlying values are, which determine our group behavior, and which help us to prioritize decisions. This is the NORM phase. Who will do what, when and where, how will we relate to each other and to our clients and suppliers? In other words, we must agree on our BEHAVIORS.

Finally, we can go out and PERFORM as a coherent and professional team, every player knowing which part they are expected to play and what their teammates will be doing.

Obviously, creating a HPT involves more than simply declaring a common mission and values. The manager who said, "there seems to be a gap between what we say our values are, and what we actually do in practice" has identified the missing link: the values do not translate into BEHAVIORS. The SABRe model illustrates the shortfall.

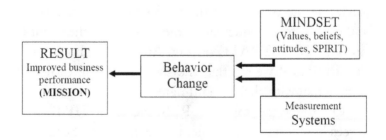

The desired RESULT is expressed in the Mission Statement. A generic Mission statement, such as displayed in many Reception walls, says something like: "be the best supplier of A in market B". This is largely useless, unless we SPECIFY, QUANTIFY what we mean by "Best". Jack Welch, ex-CEO of General Electric, defined it as "being the No. 1 or No. 2 company in the market as measured by sales."

It is easy enough to set up a measuring SYSTEM to verify if we are No. 1 or No. 2 in the market.

What BEHAVIOR can generate this result?

Welch suggested: "if we are not in the Top two, either: fix it, sell it, or close it."

Welch made the desired behaviors sound easy: he had a talent for communicating. The most difficult part of designing an HPT is defining the BEHAVIORS.

For example: many companies state that one of their central values is RESPECT.

What behaviors demonstrate that the manager is living the value of RESPECT?

An example: a manager is consistently late, habitually keeping his subordinates waiting. While he may say that he respects them, his behavior tells a different story. Time is more than money, it is LIFE. Any manager that does not value the time – and the lives - of his subordinates sufficiently to be punctual in meetings with them does not DEMONSTRATE respect. And so, we should not be surprised if we see that the subordinates in turn are unpunctual with their subordinates.

On the same topic of RESPECT, an **HPT** also agrees how it handles conflict between its members. The next chapter offers some insights.

People mirror the behaviors of their leaders, more than the declared values.

21

PERFORMING as a High-Performance Team

In the previous chapter, we stated that defining the BEHAVIORS of a High-Performance Team is one of the most difficult tasks. This chapter provides more light on the topic.

The book "Positivity" by Dr. Barbara L. Fredrickson is a worthwhile read. She recounts her collaboration with Dr. Marcial Losada, a Chilean-born psychologist and mathematician. Losada spent years observing business teams, to determine those characteristics which differentiated high performing teams from ordinary teams. He tracked three dimensions in business meetings, quantifying whether the team member's statements were:

(1) based on ENQUIRY (asking questions) as opposed to ADVOCACY (stating a point of view)
(2) SELF-FOCUSED (talking about "myself" and / or "us") as opposed to OTHER-FOCUSED (talking about "they", the others)
(3) POSITIVE or NEGATIVE.

Losada found two striking features of high performing teams.

The first characteristic was that they displayed what he calls "connectivity". By this, he means that there is a balance between Enquiry and Advocacy, and Self-Focus Other-Focus. In other words, team members on HPT's asked questions as much as they defended their own views, and they cast their attention outward as much as inward.

The second was that high performing teams had unusually high positivity ratios (the ratio of positive to negative comments). Typically, 6 or 7 to 1. Poor-performing teams had a ratio of 1 to 1 or less. Mixed-performance teams sat around 2 to 1.

Losada later calculated the "tipping point", the ratio at which teams started to transform from middling to high-performance. It is 2.71 to 1. He calls this the "Losada Line". For practical purposes, it means that **a team must have at least 3 positives for each negative** just to START flying as a high-performing team.

Extreme negativity causes teams to lose their good cheer, their ability to question, each person simply defends their own position and becomes critical of others. Unfortunately, 30% of the teams Losada observed fell into this type.

25% were high-performing teams, the remainder mixed-performance.

Losada's and Fredrickson's work has helped bring attention to the importance of behavior in business meetings.

We can use this to suggest three very specific behaviors for highly productive teams:

1. We ask questions of others at the same rate as we defend our own viewpoints.
2. We speak about ourselves, internally, at the same rate as we speak about others, externally.
3. We make more than **four** positive comments for every negative comment.

22

Motivating Employees for Productivity

In previous chapters, we covered why employees should set their own personal and professional goals as a route towards maximizing their personal productivity. In this chapter, we discuss how companies can interact with employees to harness this productivity in a mutually beneficial way.

MESHING ORGANIZATIONAL & PERSONAL MISSIONS

Employees have their personal goals, and the organization has its goals, commonly expressed as its "Mission". Managers must demonstrate to employees that their career achievements and personal development goals are intertwined with their contribution to the organization's mission.

At the core of a person's self-esteem is the achievement of noble objectives, whether individually or as part of a team. Employee satisfaction comes from public recognition of purposeful and meaningful work that makes a positive contribution.

One of a manager's responsibilities is to maximize potential for motivation. This means providing opportunities to reach the self-actualization apex of Maslow's Pyramid. At the top of the Pyramid is our drive to learn, to improve our environment, to help others, to gain recognition and to contribute to the common good. We, as managers, are duty bound to create a work environment in which employees can grow professionally and personally. And also – the same is true for us!

POSITIVE USE OF EXPECTANCY

Imagine for a moment that you are an infant again. Imagine how you felt, the incredible motivating power running through you as you see the look of expectancy on your parent's face when you are taking your very first steps. That look motivates you through the risk and pain of failure. Your parents' joy and laughter overcome your initial tendency to cry when you fall over and give you the courage to stand up on your own two feet once again.

As adults, we still have the same programming that causes us to seek that same positive encouragement. We all long for that look that sees the best in us, forgives our failures, and encourages us to be strong, robust, joyful, and creative. Employees long for that look in the eyes of their supervisor or manager – the special look that reminds them that they have something of value to give, that their potential for excellence is just below the surface.

THREE SIMPLE GUIDELINES FOR MOTIVATING

1. **Replace criticism with an environment of safety and respect.**
   Catch people doing something right, as described in "The One-Minute Manager". Effective leaders find several positive things to point out in an employee's work alongside every suggestion for improvement.

2. **Replace coercion with choice.**
   No manager can force an individual employee to grow professionally or personally. You can only create the environment and extend the invitation. Offering a choice will avoid the resistance usually encountered with the implied threat and pressure of "you have to". "Mechanical" compliance will gain half-hearted obedience, but full commitment is more likely when we feel we have a choice and an opportunity to contribute to a higher good.

3. **Replace crisis management with clear vision.**
   Everyone from the General Manager to the cleaning lady needs to understand the Company's Mission and how to use it to define priorities. Without a clearly understood common purpose, low priority tasks and bureaucratic rules divert us from our objectives, creating activity, not productivity.

23

A fun Productivity Audit

Just for fun, take this productivity audit questionnaire into your Company or Department.

		Self-Assessment: **Highly Productive Culture**	Yes	No
RESULTS	In your company, do you know:	how much is the optimum profit?		
		how much profits increase if you raise productivity by 20%?		
		the percentage of activities which add value to your clients?		
		the percentage of lost sales and why?		
BEHAVIORS	In your company, do you observe that your people:	avoid or postpone decision making?		
		copy you and everybody with emails?		
		spend a lot of time writing reports which explain failures?		
		wait for you to take decisions for them?		
		react to a crisis, instead of planning calmly?		
		everything appears urgent, due yesterday?		
SYSTEMS	In your company, is it possible to know:	the productivity in every area, every day?		
		the performance at the bottleneck area?		
		progress against the plan each hour?		
		the reasons for not achieving the plan every day?		
		these reasons quantified and ranked for action?		
		the corrective actions in order of importance?		
ATTITUDES	In your company, do many people think like this:	"it's not my job, it's the other area or shift"?		
		"if I say what I think, my boss will admonish me "?		
		"if you want something well done, you better do it yourself"?		
		"improving by 20% is almost impossible"?		
		"the only way to improve is to invest or spend more money"?		
		"if you want me to produce more, you'll have to pay me more"?		

You may also wish to add these general questions:

1. *What is your company's definition of productivity? Does it consider only that which gives VALUE ADDED to the client?*

2. *Which of your departments or areas is more productive?*

3. *Does your company have a true measure of its productivity losses, the Mudas?*

4. *Does your company have a true measure of customer service?*

5. *Does your company have a work procedure that permits optimizing the use of management and supervisory time?*

6. *Do your employees contribute with their passion and intuitive intelligence to the success of the business?*

7. *Does your company have productive meetings that are clearly focused on actions and results?*

Do not be discouraged if the answers are not as great as you would have hoped. You have just found out some good news. You have identified some opportunities for improvements in your company's productivity and profits.

If you come out with a perfect score sheet, your company has no further room for improvement, so better polish up your résumé now!

24

Common mistakes in productivity measurement

A ny business owner or manager will recognize that there is a close relationship between the productivity of his business and its profitability. So therefore, to increase profitability, a logical route is to improve productivity. But, only 15% of companies have meaningful productivity indicators as part of their management information systems.

We must choose our measurement mechanisms with great care. Dr. Steven Covey said, "sometimes when we work so hard to climb the ladder of success, we don't realize until we finally get to the top that the ladder has been supported against the wrong wall all this time."

Studies have shown that as many as 85% of companies either do not have productivity indices as part of their management information systems, or even if they do possess productivity indicators, these are so misleading as to cause management often to take incorrect decisions. The most common mistakes in measuring productivity are:

1. **The error of omission; simply not measuring at all.**
   A company which does not measure its productivity can only improve by luck or great difficulty.

2. **Measuring the wrong thing in a manufacturing environment.**
   A company with, say 20 dissimilar products, typically adds up the units of each and relates the total to the number of resources used. For example, in week one, the manager says to his staff, "20 apples and 30 oranges, give 50 units divided by 50 man-hours worked, gives 1 unit per man-hour. Well done!"

   The manager totally ignores the fact that apples take three times as long as oranges to process. So, in week 2, there is no demand for oranges, so the staff dedicate the time to apples instead. Instead of making 30 oranges, they can make 10 apples (because apples take three times as long as oranges!). Therefore, the manager says, "30 apples and 0 oranges give 30 units, divided by 50 man-hours worked, gives 0.6 units per man-hour. What the #"*$*# is going on here? Heads are going to roll!"

3. **Measuring the wrong thing in a service company.**
   Sometimes a manager will take pride on his ability to manage his people by assigning deadlines and following up on them. He gives John and Peter 5 tasks each, all with a deadline for Friday, two weeks hence. When he sits down at the end of the period with each of them, he is pleased to see that John has completed all his five tasks. "Well done, John". John had in fact finished all his tasks the previous Tuesday.

When the Manager turns to Peter, he finds that Peter has only completed three of the assigned tasks. "What the #"*$*# is going on here, Peter? Pull your socks up, like John!"

The Manager has overlooked the fact that Peter had completed three assignments all designed to increase the value of the service that the company supplies to its clients, and the two others were internal administrative matters of little real import to a client. Furthermore, the manager is also oblivious to the fact that *all* of John's assignments were internal bureaucratic procedures, with no positive benefit for the company's clients, whereas the three assignments completed by Peter's were crucial to the company's competitive position.

If the manager had measured the workload assigned to each, the manager would have seen that the workload requested from Peter was double the amount of hours required from John.

4. **If employees are paid according to a variable salary, the manager will assume they will be so motivated to look after their own productivity, and therefore the manager does not have to get involved in their motivation.**

    In production areas, this is called payment by "piecework", while in service industries, we use the term "commissions". So, when a manager sees that his or her people look busy, the manager assumes that everything is fine. This is not management, but abdication of management to a payment system. The manager fails to see is that *activity* is not the same as *productivity.* Just because a person is active, does not necessarily mean that he is productive. Quite often, the reverse is true.

5. **Incorrect paradigms regarding productivity. Here are some examples:**

- *"It's too difficult to measure productivity here, and the result would not be worth the effort."*
- *"The work here is too variable."*
- *"Our business is very seasonal."*
- *"We measure ourselves against deadlines; it's practically the same thing."*
- *"Productivity measures are not applicable to our type of business."*
- *"Our people are all professionals, we trust them to always do their best, and so we do not need to measure their productivity."*
- *"We pay per piece (or commission) so we do not have to worry about the productivity of our people, because their result directly affects their pockets."*
- *"We just do not know (or do not understand) how to apply the concepts of productivity here."*
- *"It would take too much paperwork."*
- *"It would take too much time."*
- *"We don't have the resources."*
- *"It's not worth the while, because our capacity is fixed and exceeds our demand."*
- *"There is a resistance or fear against measurements of that type since we laid off some people some time ago."*

These misperceptions are often accompanied by real productivity levels (unknown to the managers) of between 35% and 60%. Consequently, many of the following operational problems exist in companies:

1. *Long and stressful working hours*
2. *Poor levels of customer service*
3. *Passive supervisory styles*
4. *High levels of observed activity, but low levels of real productivity: "we are so busy, but it appears that we are not advancing much".*
5. *Project deadlines often not met.*
6. *Costs exceed budgets.*
7. *Unclear priorities- everything is urgent and due yesterday*
8. *Atmosphere of uncertainty and fear*
9. *Excessive workloads for some, light workloads for others*
10. *Lack of discipline in meetings resulting in much time lost*
11. *Excessive communication of unnecessary information to inappropriate persons*
12. *Culture of "cover my ass" memos*
13. *Duplicated and/or unclear responsibilities*

If you find five or more instances in your company, then you have received good news: by attacking these problems, you would be not only improving the productivity and motivation in your business, but also its profitability. However, for it to work smoothly, you must do it in an atmosphere of respect and participation.

This means working WITH the employees and workforce, making them participants in the process. Do that and "resistance to change" will disappear like mist under the sun.

25

Calculate the extra profit you can achieve with a 20% productivity increase

All companies measure their sales. But: how many measure their lost sales? Very few measure the number of sales that they failed to realize due to not delivering the product or service in a timely manner, or delivering incomplete services, or with quality failures. And, of the few that do measure their lost sales, many do not measure the CAUSES.

To increase profits, people often think of increasing sales. But, if the costs increase in the same proportion, we lose the opportunity to earn the profits we should have earned.

Another route is to increase sales AND IMPROVE PRODUCTIVITY. There are many instances where a productivity enhancement program has led to sales increases because lead times, order fulfillment rates, and product quality are improved. This leads to happy salespeople, with more commissions and no need for motivational courses to increase sales!

Let's calculate how much additional profit can be generated from a 20% increase in productivity. For the purposes of this example, we assume a company with the following characteristics:

- ❖ A company with US$11 million sales annually, $10 million costs, $1 million profit
- ❖ The 20% productivity increase comes from increasing sales by 20% without increasing costs proportionately
- ❖ Raw materials account for 50% of costs, direct labor 15%, indirect personal and fixed costs 35%.
- ❖ Let's leave aside as a safety margin any improvement in materials yield (scrap reduction, rejects, rework, etc.)

To achieve this, our goals are:

- reduce delivery times,
- improve quality,
- fulfill the exact quantities of customers' orders, in the moment they ask for them.

Example of Profit increase from Productivity Change			
US$ Millions			
	Pre	Post	% Improvement
Sales	11	13,2	20%
Raw Materials	5	6	
Direct labor	1,5	1,8	20%
		increase for productivity bonus, not headcount	
Fixed Costs, Admin. Etc.	3,5	3,5	
Total Costs	10	11,3	
Gross Profit	1,0	1,9	90%

In this simplified example, **a 20% productivity increase leads to a 90% jump in profitability.**

Recommendation: do this exercise for your own department or Company.

26

Should you improve productivity across the whole Company?

The intuitive answer to this question is "YES".

In the previous chapter, we saw an example where a 20% productivity improvement generated a 90% profits increase. A valuable result. Do you need to work in every single department in the Company to generate such a worth-while result?

The good news is normally, no.

We can take advantage of another of nature's laws. We know that every chain has a weakest link. If you pull on a multi-link chain, it will eventually break, but not everywhere, just at one link: the weakest link. The same applies true for any process. A process is a sequence of activities. Often, we will find that there is one activity which restricts the performance of the entire process. If we find this constraining activity, and liberate it, we can improve the capacity of the whole process.

This comes from the work of Dr. Eli Goldratt, as explained in his powerful book, "The Goal", recommended reading. He refers to his methodology as the "Theory of Constraints".

Here is a simplified example of the Theory of Constraints in action.

We have a process, consisting of 5 activities, A, B, C, D and E, performed by Alan, Bill, Charlie, Derek, and Erica respectively, before the result is sent to the Customer:

Alan → Bill → Charlie → Derek → Erica → Customer

The activities A to E are different, and so require different amounts of time to complete each one:

Activity	A →	B →	C →	D →	E
Minutes / activity	3	2	6	5	4

Take a few minutes to answer these three questions:

1. How many services can this process deliver in one hour?

2. If the 5 colleagues all work ONLY 8 hours per day exclusively on this process, and we assume zero lost time (smoke and toilet breaks, etc.) what is the maximum services that can be delivered per day?

3. You must recommend between two investments. A US$10,000 investment can improve Alan's process time to 1 minute. Or: A US$50,000 investment can improve Charlie's process time to 4 minutes.
   Which would you recommend?

Answers:

Activity	A →	B →	C →	D →	E
Minutes / activity	3	2	6	5	4
Activities / Hour	20	30	10	12	15

At 100% output, C can only produce 10 per hour. This is therefore the maximum that this process can deliver. The other activities will always have idle time. Activity C is the restriction.

In 8 hours, assuming 100% output, the maximum obtained by this process is 80.

Spending US$10,000 to reduce Alan's time from 3 minutes to 1 minute will have ZERO impact on the overall process – Alan will merely have more lost time. Spending US$50,000 to reduce Charlie's time from 6 minutes to 4 minutes will give a 20% increase for the overall process – Charlie will now be able to produce 15 per hour, but the whole team can now produce 12 per hour, as the bottleneck now becomes Derek.

27

Use psychology to improve productivity

A widely held belief among managers is that whatever you measure improves. This is true not only for businesses, but for personal interests. If you are training for a marathon, by keeping a record of the times of your training runs, you improve your performance because your increased awareness spurs you on to improve.

The notion that what you measure improves is not just a hopeful idea: it actually has a well-documented foundation from a set of controlled psychological experiments done in the 1930's, at a plant belonging to General Electric. The results of these experiments are called the "Hawthorn Effect", named after the plant's location. The following account paraphrases what happened.

A group of psychologists wished to study the effect of changing environments on the productivity of the people working in the Hawthorn plant. As they caused different changes in the environment, they observed that productivity levels continually rose. For example, they first increased the lighting levels, only to observe that productivity increased. Pleased with this finding, they then added soft background music, and were even more pleased to see that productivity increased even further. Then, someone suggested brightening up the walls with a fresh coat of pastel-colored paint, which was duly done. Our psychologist friends were delighted to observe that productivity increased yet again.

Just as they were relishing in the thought of how famous they were going to be, and how these experiments were brilliant material for their doctoral theses, one of the group had a disturbing thought: "Hold on a minute. Something external unknown to us may have caused these improvements. If what we have done are sure-fire ways to increase productivity, then it would make sense that if we were to return everything to its original state, then the productivity levels should drop to around their original levels, right?"

After some reluctant mutterings, they group agreed that he was probably right. And so, they removed the painting, the music, and the lights, returning the plant to its original state. But this time, the outcome dumbfounded the group. Instead of dropping as predicted in the model, productivity rose again!

As you can imagine, this unexpected result caused some moments of panic and some rapid revisions of working theories. Finally, the group identified that the change that had really caused the productivity improvements was the fact that the productivity was being measured and that the people were aware of the level of interest being shown towards them. Not only were the people reacting to the positive interest directed towards them, but more importantly, they could also see the results of what they were doing on the productivity indicator.

This experience has since been repeated many times across the globe. In our experience as productivity improvement engineers, we often see that implementing a productivity measurement system will result in an 8% to 10% rise in as little as two weeks. People generally like having objective feedback about how productive they are being.

This chapter starts with the statement, "what you measure improves". The opposite is also true: "What you don't measure, doesn't exist." If simply measuring productivity can generate an improvement, can your company really afford not to measure it?

What does an 8 - 10% productivity increase do to your profits?

28

How to Find Gold in your Company

You are by now familiar with the concept of Muda. For those readers who like to jump from chapter to chapter, and who may be dipping into this chapter first, a quick recap is in order. Muda is a Japanese word used to describe everything that happens within a company which fails to add value to the product or service for the client.

Finding Muda in a company is like finding a gold vein in a mine. When confronted honestly and openly, the Muda provides a rich source of additional profits through increased productivity, better customer service, and better quality.

Here is an approach for filtering out these gold nuggets or Muda. We will take the example of a hypothetical salesman, whose activities in a typical day include, 'visit customer', 'write meeting report', 'travel to client or back to office', or 'telephone client to set meeting', or 'process order'. Simply ask these 5 following questions with respect to each activity or event. For example, let us take the first activity, 'visit customer'.

The first filter is: Can the activity be eliminated? In this case of a salesman, face-to-face contact between people may be important. Can it be done remotely? If it were a case of sales of simple products or commodities, you could consider eliminating the activity through an Internet ordering system.

The second filter is: Can the activity be combined with other activities? You may wish for the salesman to assume some debt collection activities, or to check the client's inventory, or to adapt the design of the product for the client, or to produce the order form during the meeting itself, instead of afterwards, sitting in his car.

The third filter is: Can the activity be modified to reduce its time? You may believe or suspect that 60 minutes for a sales visit is too long, and upon investigating further, you discover that the salesman allows 60 minutes for each meeting, because on average his customers keep him waiting from 20 minutes to half an hour. You dig further, and you find that invariably the customers who keep him waiting are usually those with whom he has not arranged the meeting by telephone prior to leaving his office. So, one of the things you instigate is that the salesman confirms every meeting by telephone and email the day before.

The fourth filter is: Can the activity be automated? The answer is probably no, but you could consider receiving orders for standard goods and services over the internet.

The fifth filter is: Can the activity be delegated to an employee of lower cost? Or externalized? Here, you investigate with the Pareto Effect, and you find that the salesman spends the same amount of time with his 10 key customers, which represent 80% of his sales, as he does with the 40 others, which only represent 20% of his sales. So, in addition to helping him reprogram his time to dedicate more time to his key accounts, you could take the smallest accounts and assign them to a recently recruited junior salesman, for example.

So, you can see that these "filters" are a tool which allows you to focus your questions, as you seek to eliminate or reduce the effect of each activity. In this way, you will be able to catch 80% of the Muda gold nuggets and increase your company's bottom-line.

29

Improving performance of IT areas

*A*rtificial deadlines create stress and lower productivity.
Learn how to renegotiate and manage them.

A major insurance company requested a survey to
find out how other companies in the financial services
industry structured their IT departments (whether by
type of technology, business area, or by projects), how they
measured the performance of their IT areas, and whether
the structure used had a noticeable effect on performance.
The survey sample covered some 22 companies, including
major UK and USA banking and insurance operations,
along with the larger companies in Chile.

The study showed that the main method for measuring
performance was against Gantt Chart deadlines. Many
participating managers were convinced that this is
the only way to measure performance in IT areas. The
concept of productivity measurement was alien to most
of the interviewees.

We could find no relationship between performance
and the type of structure chosen. Nor was there a
connection between the level of perceived stress and the

structure. However, practically all respondents reported high perceived levels of stress.

It appeared that the high perceptions of stress reported were linked to the fact that the principal form of performance measurement was against deadlines. This led to the question: does there exist a more effective way of performance measurement for an IT area, a way which will not only measure and allow for increased performance, while simultaneously reducing stress levels?

Yes. When we incorporate productivity principles into the management control system for IT areas, we can achieve a productivity improvement with an associated reduction in stress. The following example shows why this is so.

Let us imagine Fred and Barney, two employees in Mid-Life Insurance's IT department. At the end of each month, they meet with their boss, Wilma, who uses the opportunity to review their performance, and assigns the tasks for the coming month. At the end of June, Wilma assigns three projects each to Fred and Barney, as shown in the following table:

PROJECT ASSIGNMENT SHEET June			
Project	Assigned to:		Deadline date
	Fred	Barney	
A	✓		31 July
B		✓	31 July
C	✓		31 July
D		✓	31 July
E	✓		31 July
F		✓	31 July
			TOTALS
Projects assigned	3	3	6
Mandays available	25	25	50

Wilma tells the two analysts that she will meet again with them at the end of the following month, July, when she expects them to report to her that all 6 projects are completed. A clear example of management by deadlines, wouldn't you say?

As soon as he gets back to his work area, Barney gets a phone call, from Betty, the Commercial Director. She is the client or recipient of project B, which has been assigned to Barney. She is calling him to stress the importance of this project, which will almost certainly lead to an increase in sales, as it will allow the life insurance sales force to propose to their clients the range of Mid-Life's general insurance products, and vice versa for the general insurance sales force.

The month passes, and Fred and Barney go to meet up with Wilma. Fred is relaxed, because he completed his three assignments by the 20th, and spent the time left looking busy, "doing background research on the Web". However, Barney is a bundle of nerves. He has completed only one job, project D, and still needs a week to finish the important sales project B for Betty, reckoning that he is only 80% advanced. He has encountered unexpected problems from the prospective users and has been held up, as on many occasions as either they did not give him the full amount of time he required from them, or they simply failed to show up for their scheduled meetings with him. To Barney's amazement, the future end users of the system he was designing appeared to have little interest in his attempts to make their lives easier or better! It was almost as if they did not know about the project he was trying to develop for them! As he felt an emotional commitment to Betty, and had given his promise to her, he battled on, nonetheless. He had spent many nights in the office until 10pm, and even worked during some of his weekends on this project. Given the lack of progress, he had worked the previous two nights until midnight. Despite his efforts, he knows that Wilma will focus on the two projects he did not do, rather than on the one that he did complete. He knows from experience that Wilma only focuses on the results, not on the reasons for failure. He knows that she expects highly educated professionals to be able to manage their work within the time available to produce the desired results.

True to form, Wilma warmly congratulates Fred, and gives Barney a verbal roasting. "Only 1 out of 3 projects completed within the deadline? Disgraceful performance! Why can't you be more like Fred? He met his deadlines! Your lack of performance makes me look bad to my boss. See, thanks to you, my area performance is only 67%! And all of the overtime was spent on you!" Wilma hands her Monthly Report to Barney, who sees:

Both Barney and Fred come out stressed from the meeting. As far as Barney is concerned, the reason is obvious: the recent grilling. But Fred has two reasons to feel stressed, as well. Not only does he feel embarrassed because he knows that the comparison Wilma made between his performance and Barney's is unrealistic, but also, he knows that the next time around, with Wilma's arbitrary system of assigning projects, he may well be on the receiving end of a lashing from Wilma's acidic tongue.

IT AREA PERFORMANCE REPORT				
June				
Project	Assigned to:		Deadline date	Completed?
	Fred	Barney		
A	✓		31 July	Yes
B		✓	31 July	NO
C	✓		31 July	Yes
D		✓	31 July	Yes
E	✓		31 July	Yes
F		✓	31 July	NO

				TOTALS
Projects Completed	PLAN	3	3	6
	ACTUAL	3	1	4
	% PERFORMANCE	100%	33%	67%
Mandays Worked	PLAN	25	25	50
	ACTUAL	25	35	60
	Overtime Mandays	-	10	10
Mandays / Project	PLAN	8,3	8,3	8,3
	ACTUAL	8,3	35,0	15,0

What are the weaknesses with Wilma's method? Here are some:

- **There is no attempt to match the volume of work required to the resources available.**

    Consequently, there is **excessive lost time** as Fred does not have enough work to stretch him, and **excessive stress** as Barney has more work than he can reasonably do in a month. The fact that there is no system to match the volume of work required to the resources available means that it will always be the case that while one person is overloaded, another person will be under-tasked.
- **The supervisory style is passive.**

At no time during the month did Wilma follow up to see how her analysts were doing against their targets. Consequently, there is also **excessive lost time** incurred by Barney, who was obliged to waste an enormous amount of time waiting for his project's end users to provide the input he needed. If Wilma had spoken to Barney every 2 days or so after handing out the assignments, she would have detected this problem, and she would have spoken to Betty to remind her to make sure that her people made time for Barney to incorporate their concerns into his design.

A question remains: what is it about Wilma's style that Barney did not feel enough confidence to report a problem to her before their monthly meeting?

- **There is no prioritizing of projects** in terms of which add more value to the client, and therefore to the company.

  Because the main indicator of production is "projects finished", as a result, the easiest or quickest or the least important jobs were worked on first, and the most important project became overdue, with the consequent lack of sales for the company.

- As a result of all of the above, the **customer service level is poor**.

  In the case of Wilma, only 67% (4 out of her 6 customers) received their projects within the promised time.

All of this could have been avoided had Wilma incorporated productivity principles into her deadline management system. Let us look at what could have happened.

Wilma has identified six projects which need to be done. Her first task will be to rate the value-adding benefit offered by each project. Her decision ranks the projects in order, with a percent rating against each, as follows:

Project	B	F	D	C	E	A
Rating %	81%	70%	65%	40%	25%	15%

Her next task is to estimate the work content of each project, in man-days for an analyst, assuming he or she were to work on each project with 100% dedication. This looks as follows:

Project	B	F	D	C	E	A
Estimated man-days	30	70	65	40	25	15

After this, she assigns the projects to her analysts, starting with the most important and working down. She also considers whether the work can reasonably be spread across one person, and if so, she decides to assign the work to both analysts to work together as a team in order to accelerate the delivery time to the client.

Putting these three steps together, her Project Assignment Sheet now looks like:

			IT AREA MONTHLY PLAN June			
Project	Value Added Priority	Estimated Mandays	Assigned to:		Deadline date
			Fred	Barney	
A	1	30	15	15	19 July
B	2	5	5		25 July
C	3	2	1	1	22 July
D	4	7		7	22 July
E	5	5	5		29 July
F	6	3		3	31 July

TOTALS	52	26	26
Available mandays	50	25	25
Overtime authorized	2	1	1

But the fact that Wilma is using a better system does not by itself help her to improve the performance of Fred and Barney, and hence that of her area. She also needs to change something about herself. The first thing she needs to change is her belief that professionally educated people are like automats, that you can give them an instruction, and not expect to see them until the allotted time has expired, at which time all you have to do is to review the results.

As part of the new system, Wilma should follow the adage, "even good people need following up." Wilma makes it a point of principle that she will enquire as to the progress of each project at every 10% interval, in other words, every 2 days or so.

So, after a day and a half, she approaches Barney and Fred, to find out how they are getting on. They explain to her, the end users appear to have little interest in the new system, that they seem to not know why they are asking them all these questions. Wilma suspects that the real problem is that Betty has forgotten to inform her staff that some IT personnel would be coming around asking questions, and their collaboration is necessary. She arranges for a quick informal meeting with Betty. Betty, overworked as usual, apologizes for the lack of communication with her people, and promises to correct the situation that very afternoon.

The next time Barney and Fred go to the Commercial Area, they are received warmly. They quickly get the information they need, develop the new system, and finish it within the 30 man-days allocated.

At the end of the month, the department performance appears as follows:

IT AREA PERFORMANCE REPORT						
			June			
Project	Value Added Priority	Estimated Mandays	Assigned to:		Deadline date	Completed?
			Fred	Barney		
A	1	30	15	15	19 July	Yes
B	2	5	5		25 July	Yes
C	3	2	1	1	22 July	Yes
D	4	7		7	22 July	Yes
E	5	5	5		29 July	Yes
F	6	3		3	31 July	Yes

TOTALS	52	26	26	
Available mandays	50	25	25	
Overtime authorized	2	1	1	

Projects Completed	PLAN	3	3	6
	ACTUAL	3	3	6
	% PERFORMANCE	100%	100%	100%
Mandays worked	PLAN	26	26	52
	ACTUAL	26	26	52
	Overtime days	1	1	2
Mandays / Project	PLAN	8,7	8,7	8,7
	ACTUAL	8,7	8,7	8,7

The results of this approach are summarized in the following table:

	BEFORE	AFTER	% Change
Projects completed	4	6	50%
Estimated Man-days EARNED *assuming 80% of Project B completed BEFORE*	41	52	27%
Mandays worked	60	52	-13%
Mandays Overtime	10	2	-80%
Productivity: Estimated Mandays EARNED / Mandays worked	0,68	1,0	46%

The new method gives Wilma a 46% increase in departmental productivity, with a 13% reduction in days worked, an 80% reduction in overtime and a 27% increase in effective work done.

But there are other intangible benefits, which are probably more important. Her analysts are achieving more, while under less stress, and Wilma now has a fairer system for objectively measuring the respective performance of her two analysts.

30

How to achieve Highly Productive Maintenance

*I*n *this Chapter, we assume that Highly Productive Production and Planning are in place. Highly Productive Maintenance can only exist together and in harmony with Highly Productive Production and Highly Productive Planning. One alone cannot exist without the other two.*

There are 8 steps to achieving a Highly Productive Maintenance operation, following the SABRe method, previously mentioned in Chapter 1. They are:

Step One: Understand the current situation through a system analysis

In order to understand how far short we are from Highly Productive Maintenance, we need to do first analyze in-depth the current systems and procedures, covering: maintenance crew planning, the work order system, planning and scheduling the 3 families of maintenance activities (preventive maintenance, repairs and project works), inventory control and the purchasing system, management reporting, and automation.

The way we do this is to map out visually the current flow of maintenance information, taking the life cycle of a representative work order. This means reviewing the role of every employee in the maintenance process and putting every activity into a flow chart, and including whatever measurements are currently used to determine the effectiveness of the department and its interactions with other departments.

Step Two: Understand the current situation: behavioral analysis

After gaining an understanding of the current system, it is necessary to understand how people work in it, how maintenance and production interact. This is best achieved by doing a series of live observations to learn what hinders the maintenance people from accomplishing their daily tasks. Spending full shifts with the technicians allows us to see the work from their viewpoint, and allows us to quantify the percentages of their day spent adding value, performing non-value-added tasks or idly waiting for instructions or something to happen.

Step Three: Understand the current situation: problems and opportunities

The work done in the previous two steps is now brought together and analyzed to identify the weaknesses or opportunities. Often, we find at least one, if not several of the following characteristics:

- **There is no objective measure of maintenance productivity.**
  Instead, a typical maintenance manager uses a "gut-feel" or subjective measurement approach. If he assigns a job to Barney Rubble, he expects it to be done by lunchtime, but if he assigns it Fred Flintstone, he won't expect to see the completed job until the end of the week. The manager considers that productivity measurements are okay for production, but as maintenance is a "craft / artisan" area, such concepts do not apply. If he does use a measurement, it may be something like "Maintenance costs-per-production unit", but such a measure is usually meaningless, as product mixes change due to seasonal variations. Hence, he does not feel accountable if this index increases.

- **Detailed historical machine maintenance and repair records are lacking.**
  As maintenance technicians usually regard themselves as skilled artists and tend to avoid anything which smacks of performance measurement, they resist the non-glamorous administrative part of their job, recording sketchy details at best. Records are not centralized or easily accessible, so that

predictive maintenance practices based on historical failures are difficult to develop.

• **There is little coordination between Production and Maintenance Planning.** Production constantly deviates from agreed plans to make certain machines available for maintenance, because of sales pressures. Hence weekly maintenance plans become meaningless. Capacity Planning for Production doesn't consider maintenance requirements or maintenance capacity.

• **Maintenance productivity is low.** Technicians may be extremely active, scurrying from one fire-fighting emergency to another, but this hides a low productivity. Quite often, we find that the time spent adding value is well below 50% of a technician's day.

• **Poor maintenance inventory control.** Some not-so-key parts have years of inventory cover, while other key items are constantly suffering stock outages. Hence both maintenance costs and production downtime will be higher than they need to be.

• **Passive management and supervisory styles.** Even though the Manager or Supervisor assigns jobs to Barney Rubble and Fred Flintstone, he does not have a formal system for following up on the work assigned. In

Barney's case, he expects the job to be done by lunchtime, but when Barney has problems and finishes just before shift end, the supervisor is unaware of the drop in performance and the reasons for it.

- **Haphazard Repair and Maintenance Planning.**

  All too often, Work Orders are issued simply assuming that the required parts or materials are available in stock. When they are not, not only does production downtime increase, but also maintenance time increases as does the backlog of overdue work. In many cases there is no system for assigning estimated man-hours, skill levels, parts required or even priority levels for Work Orders. This sometimes results in technicians choosing their Work Orders based on personal preferences, rather than company needs.

- **Inadequate Preventative Maintenance and Shutdown Planning.**

  Planned shutdown times for major overhauls typically overrun; outside contractors are often left unsupervised. This leads to far longer downtime for production. And because of the passive supervisory culture, little real analysis of the shutdown is done afterwards to determine causes and magnitudes of the problems which resulted in the delays.

Step Four: Create a Maintenance Mission and Design a new Highly Productive System

Using the results from the previous in-depth analysis, we agree on a Vision and Mission for Maintenance, then design a new Maintenance Planning, Control and management Reporting System through involving all the key staff. Here we use the 5 filters mentioned in Chapter 28.

Involving the employees in developing a better system is crucial. Once they have helped design the new system, which should also make their work easier and better, they are more willing to buy into the changes.

This step also requires three specific types of training: team formation; productivity and lean manufacturing concepts; and user training with the new systems. The teams agree to a specific set of new behaviors which they will adopt with the new system, principally a commitment to adopt a proactive supervisory style.

Step Five: Install the new system in a Pilot Area as a "dry run"

To detect and design out any wrinkles in the new system, we may choose a particular shutdown, or production area, or even one maintenance team (mechanical, electrical, preventive, etc.) to work with the new system during a few weeks. Once the bugs are identified and cleared out, and it is clear that the new system can replace the old one without any further major glitches, the old system drops away and the entire area is working to the new methods and procedures.

Where should we start? Why not start with the bottlenecks in the process? Chapter 26.

Step Six: Extend the new System to other areas

Typical results which can be achieved are:

- Increase in time spent on preventive maintenance
- Reduction in production downtime due to breakdowns
- The total time of Production taken up by • Maintenance (time spent on repairs and on preventive work) falls, giving a consequent increase in productivity for Production
- Maintenance productivity increases by 20% to 30%
- Use of overtime hours drops
- Reduction in maintenance inventories

Step Seven: Audit the new Systems for Usage

Once an improvement has been achieved, there is sometimes a tendency to "rest on the laurels", and some people start taking short cuts with the system. If this is not addressed, over time, the systems will revert to something like their original state, and the improvements will be lost. Hence the need to conduct regular and formal audits to ensure a continuous commitment to the discipline of the new systems.

Not only can the audits identify systems slippage, but also, they are useful for identifying further areas for improvements. Highly Productive maintenance is more than anything a change mindset and can be killed by the mindset of routine or complacency.

Step Eight: Computerize the new Systems

The reason why we do not start with computerization is that it doesn't really change anything that is already happening. Many people do not realize that computerization alone does not lead to substantial improvements. Maintenance productivity does not improve just because work orders are in a database instead of an admin assistant's desk. Maintenance inventories will not increase, or stock-outages decrease, unless the system for purchasing and inventory control is changed. Computerization doesn't change the culture of a maintenance area from a reactive, emergency firefighting organization to a preventive or predictive one. Without a careful analysis of the value-adding activities that are required to complete a maintenance task, without identifying the real causes of equipment failures, computerization brings no real benefits. The key is to change the process and the culture first, and then computerize it to make the process easier to manage.

31

Leading more productive meetings

I magine this: you are General Manager of a medium-sized company of 200 employees, and you are requesting approval for next year's budget. One Director raises a question. There is an item which shows a cost of US$400,000 for the year, for which you cannot say what the return to the Company will be, and in all probability some US$200,000 of that expenditure will be wasted. What is this item? It is the cost of all the time that the managers and staff in a company spend in meetings.

A typical medium-sized company of 200 employees loses US$200,000* per year because of bad meeting practices. Consider the following. Let us say that 40 employees (the most expensive!) regularly attend meetings as part of their job functions. These meetings can easily occupy half of their working time, if not more. And half of the time spent in these meetings is totally wasted (Muda, if you prefer), for many reasons, some of which we list here:

- some of the participants will arrive up to 15 minutes late
- the purpose of the meeting is poorly defined
- many attendees either are not really required at the meeting or
- fail to participate fully (which gives the same result)
- people use the meeting as a forum to air other topics or grievances not related to the purpose of the meeting
- ("by the way, as I've got you here now...")
- the meeting fails to generate action or reach a conclusion.

* *The calculation used is: 40 people x 20 hours in meetings / week x 50% wasted time x US$10 per hour (very conservative!) x 50 weeks.*

The following five actions can dramatically increase productivity in management meetings.

1. **Measure and evaluate**

    In Chapter 27, we mentioned the lesson learned from the "Hawthorne Experiment": what you measure improves. Applying this well-proven principle to control of meetings, at the end of a meeting, the Chairperson gives feedback to the attendees on how successful the meeting has been, using objective indicators along these lines:

    - Man-hours planned = 8 attendees x 1 hour 15 mins = 10 man-hours

- Man-hours actual = 9 attendees x 1 hour 30 mins = 13.5 man-hours
- Obvious Muda = 8 people x 10 minutes wait at start = 1.33 man-hours
- Meeting objectives were:
  1) to decide between X and Y proposal
  2) to review Z
- Meeting results were:
  1) no decision reached between X and Y
  2) Z reviewed as planned
- Meeting achievement = 50% (1 objective out of 2 achieved)
- Meeting efficiency = 10 man-hours planned / 13.5 man-hours actual = 74%
- **Meeting productivity** = Efficiency x Achievement = 50% x 74% = **37%**

After a few weeks of reporting such low productivity figures, professional embarrassment alone will cause the results to improve!

2. **Have a prepared agenda with objectives, topics and a planned time allocated to each.** The Chairperson's job is to ensure that the meeting sticks to this Plan.
3. **Install a bar-height table** in the meeting room, which requires the attendees to stand around the table during the meeting. This is effective for meetings which should last for 1 hour or less, and which tend to overrun.
4. If you want the meeting to last for an hour at the most, **schedule it one hour before**

lunch or 45 minutes before the end of the working day.

5. **Strong meeting Leadership,** without which none of the preceding is possible.

32

Writing more productive Minutes of Meetings

In the years BZ (before Zoom), in many Companies, the Minutes of regular management meetings often run to several pages, three to six typically, generating an expensive waste of time.

First, each attendee must read through these 3 - 6 pages, so as to decide whether the Minutes reflect a "true and fair representation" of what occurred in the previous meeting, as they will be asked to either amend the Minutes or to approve them at the start of the following meeting.

Second, much of the information recorded is irrelevant; it has no direct benefit or added value to the client. For example:

"Carpark assignment of spaces. Mr. Smith reported that he disagreed with Mr. Jones on the number of spaces to be made available for visitors, pointing out that some visitors and clients have complained that they have had to park outside in the street, with the consequent security risks involved. After some discussion, it was agreed that Mr. Robinson will record the number of visitors day by day and report back with his findings in 2 weeks' time, with his recommendations."

A much more effective and productive tool is the "**MEETING ACTION REGISTER**". The above example would simply be recorded as:

ITEM	ACTION	WHO	BY WHEN
Carpark space for visitors	Record number of daily visitors and recommend number of spaces	M.R.	14 April

This type of Meeting Record has the advantage that it focuses exclusively on the actions or results to be generated. Using this, six pages of Minutes can be reduced to one, consequently reducing the unnecessary executive reading time by 80%. More apt for our current times, the years PZ (post-Zoom)!

33

More productive use of emails

In the good old days before e-mail, it was normal for a secretary to type up a memorandum, photocopy it and send a copy to everyone on the distribution list. Because of the cost of photocopies, the number of people copied was normally limited to an "as needs to know" basis.

Nowadays, with ubiquitous e-mail, the process is much cheaper and almost instantaneous. No-one nowadays asks a secretary to type - you do it yourself. No longer do we have to worry about photocopy costs: email costs almost nothing and distribution to other people for information is simply a matter of clicking on the "Copy To" icon.

While the number of paper memos is now practically zero, the overall use of paper has increased. And the promises of dramatic productivity leaps have not been realized either. A study carried out recently in the US reported that the busiest hours for Internet access are between 2 p.m. and 4 p.m. Many employees spend 1 hour or more of company time surfing the web. The expected productivity gains did not happen.

On the specific issue of memos, whereas a typical executive probably received 15 - 20 printed memos daily, nowadays anything from 100 to 200 e-mail "memos" is usual.

This is a world-wide phenomenon. A British executive recently reported that there is a thriving culture of "copy-itis" and "not my fault-itis". *What do you mean, you were not informed? I sent you a copy of my report 3 months ago!*" Everyone copies anyone remotely related to any issue. When this executive requested a colleague not to copy him with e-mails unless there was some specific value that he could add, his colleague willingly obliged. The only problem was that about 50 other people, seeing that his name was not on the distribution list, assumed that there had been an oversight, and all courteously forwarded him a copy of the e-mail memo that he was not supposed to receive!!

In organizations where there is little trust, where fear of losing one's job is prevalent, the need to "cover ass" is a powerful influence at the moment of managing e-mails. Because the average person copies three times as many people as is necessary, there is a double time wastage for each of the persons on that distribution list.

The first waste of time is the time spent reading something where you can add no real value. Some executives must block out 2 hours or more a day simply to be able to read all the e-mails they receive. Some even consider taking a speed-reading course to be able to cope with the increased volume of material. This is like treating the symptom, instead of attacking the root cause.

The second waste of time is the time spent in moving and / or copying all these e-mails to backup files which are organized by subject matter and by sender.

Here follow some tips to help you avoid falling into the e-mail swamp, or at least managing it if you are already there.

First, inform all your subordinates and peers that you wish not to be copied with any mail unless they think that there is something of a special *value that you can add*, in which case ask them to personalize your copy, detailing to you the special value that they hope you can add. The fact that someone must tell you why he or she is copying you an e-mail should mean that at least 80% of the random or automatic copies should disappear.

Second, do the same yourself with the messages you send, especially with the people to whom you copy.

Third, and this requires more care and preparation, ask the same of your superiors, while explaining to them the meaning of the terms "Value Added to Client" and "Muda". If you are an average executive, this should save you at least 1 hour of your life a day from reading non-value-added memos.

34

Putting it all together

This is a checklist compiled from the previous chapters. Use it to help guide you on your path to being a highly productive leader.

Source	Check point	Yes	No
Ch. 5,6	Have you set your personal goals?		
Ch. 7	Have you decided to be PASSIONATE about what you are doing?		
Ch. 8	Have you clarified your personal values?		
Ch. 9	Have you identified yourself-limiting beliefs, thoughts, paradigms?		
Ch. 10	Are you 100% open to personal change?		
Ch. 11	Do you have the humility and child-like curiosity to learn new things?		
Ch. 12	Do you apply the 80-20 rule to your personal activities?		

Source	Check point	Yes	No
Ch.13	Are you aware of your professional Muda?		
Ch.14	Do you apply the 5 filters to your To-Do List?		

Ch. 15	Are you clear on your Company's goals?
Ch. 16	Does your Company have a true Customer Service measure?
Ch. 17	Does your Company treat its people so as to maximize customer service?
Ch. 18	Has your Company set clear priorities between its Values?
Ch. 19	Does your organization measure how well the managers and supervisors help people to grow?
Ch. 20	Does your Top Management Team have a clear set of defined behaviors which demonstrate living the Company's Values?
Ch. 21	Does your Top Management Team practice 3 positives MINIMUM for every negative comment?
Ch. 22	Does your organization try to mesh the individual goals of employees with its Mission and Values?
Ch. 23	Does your organization regularly conduct productivity audits?
Ch. 24	Does your organization have a clear productivity indicator based on Value-Added to the Client?
Ch. 25	Does your organization know how much a 20% productivity improvement will increase profits?
Ch. 26	Has your organization identified its bottleneck / constricting resource, and has it set up procedures to maximize its utilization?
Ch. 27	Does your organization measure its productivity?
Ch. 28	Does your organization have a measurement system for detecting and quantifying Mudas?
Ch. 29	Does your organization have a system for measuring productivity in key service areas, such as IT?

Ch. 30	Does your organization have a system for measuring productivity in maintenance areas?
Ch. 31	Does your organization measure the effectiveness of management meetings?
Ch. 32	Does your organization use Action Registers instead of wordy minutes?
Ch. 33	Does your organization limit the quantity of emails to those which add value to the client?

At this point, I should wish you "Good Luck" on your high-performance professional journey. But there is no need. You will forge your own Good Luck!
A toast to your Success and Happiness!

Recommended Reading / Listening / Watching

Books:

Author	Title
Dr. Stephen Covey	The Seven Habits of Highly Productive People
Dr. Eli Goldratt	The Goal
	Critical Chain
	It's Not Luck
Dr. Barbara Frederickson	Positivity
Napoleon Hill	Think and Grow Rich
Ken Blanchard	The One-Minute Manager
W.F. Bohan	The Hidden Power of Productivity
	Doubling the Productivity of a Start Up

Articles:

MacGregor
Who's Got the Monkey?
Foundations for Human
Engineering

Listening:

Brian Tracy   The Psychology of Achievement

Video:

Video Arts / John Cleese   The Unorganized Manager

Acknowledgements

Various people were fundamental in the creation of this book, who I would like to thank here:

Alonso Morgado

Alonso did the great favor of helping to correct the very first version of this book, alongside introducing me to the culture of the "picadas chilenas". We have a joint future Project for a future book, provisionally titled *"Doubling Student Productivity"*.

Martin Flannery & Mark Watkins

Great Friends who helped redirect the book from its original concept to a post-Covid changed world. Additionally, they pointed out that this book would be of interest to supervisors and managers and that I should direct it towards a wider audience. From this advice, the title *"Driving Change"* was born.

Raul Ponce

My business partner at Trinity read my first two books, *"The Hidden Power of Productivity"* and *"Doubling your*

Startup Productivity", texts I wrote as business novels, as I find this format very didactic. The best example in my opinion and the one that most inspired me was Goldratt's "*The Goal*". When Raul read the first draught of this third book, his words were: "You should have started with this one, dude."

Rene Tovar

Being, like me, a foreigner living for many years in Chile, you are Colombian and I European, I appreciate your great help in suggesting improvements to my text during our many delightful conversations. I also celebrate that my birthday coincides with the date of your country's national day.

Review Requested:

We'd like to know if you enjoyed the book.
Please consider leaving a review on the platform from
which you purchased the book.

CPSIA information can be obtained
at www.ICGtesting.com
Printed in the USA
BVHW061010140322
631400BV00008B/358